UNITY

UNITY

ROBERT E. MAKARA

authorHOUSE®

AuthorHouse™ LLC
1663 Liberty Drive
Bloomington, IN 47403
www.authorhouse.com
Phone: 1-800-839-8640

Published by AuthorHouse   07/02/2014

ISBN: 978-1-4969-1567-2 (sc)
ISBN: 978-1-4969-1564-1 (hc)
ISBN: 978-1-4969-1562-7 (e)

Library of Congress Control Number: 2014909611

Unless otherwise noted, the Bible version used for quotes is the New Catholic Edition of the
Holy Bible: The Old Testament—Douay Version and The New Testament—Confraternity
Edition; published by the Catholic Book Publishing Company of New York; copyright 1953.

CONTENTS

INTRODUCTION

I fear death, for the pain and suffering of it all, but more so for the eternal unknown than the temporary. I believe most people share my fear, but few have been able to confront it, identify it and share it with others. A common concern shared by most, if not all, is one unifying element that may bring us together.

I should have confidence, because I feel I have lived a pretty good life, but life has taught me that nothing can be absolutely certain. I don't know everything, if not anything. There are two sides to every issue. How do *I* know I lived a good life? I may be sadly mistaken. Maybe I have not been so good. Through ignorance or arrogance or both, I may be *vastly* mistaken. "Thou hypocrite, first cast out the beam from thy own eye, and then thou wilt see clearly to cast out the speck from thy brother's eye." Matthew: 7:5. It would be an infinite mistake to fail in my desire to reach heaven, or, perhaps even worse, end up with eternal damnation, whatever that entails.

Or maybe God is not as compassionate and forgiving as I have been led to believe. Has this been just wishful thinking? Yet, I believe, which is different than I know. All the faith in the world cannot change the truth unless God so desires. Who am I to dictate the nature of God? What is is and what isn't is not.

The dove sweeps down every one million years and brushes its wing against a 12" diameter solid steel ball, and when that ball is worn down to nothing, eternity has just begun. I've heard that somewhere. And, it is an understatement.

I don't know what Adolph Hitler was thinking when he gravitated to the idea, the fantasy, of creating a super race of humans, at the expense of all human differences, imperfections and weaknesses, a total abandonment of compassion for those who don't fit the mold. Did he believe he would some day live to see the reality of his dream? Did he think that he would survive death? What kind of eternal existence did he imagine for himself? Perhaps he thought he was doing mankind a great service by creating his master race by sacrificing the undesirable and devoting his own life in service to a dream that would be beneficial to those who survive. He died by his own doing, I guess out of fear of the consequences of paying for what he had done. Did he make his peace with God at the end? Or did he believe in despair that his failure meant the end of everything, from which there would be no further life in which justice would be met? Did he think that he had done good? Who knows what he may have been thinking during those final days.

None of us can fully understand what drove Hitler to the evil agenda that he pursued, but an intense patriotic devotion to his native Germany, the overly burdensome and unjust penalties imposed on Germany from World War I and, most of all, his excruciating temporary blindness following this war were major factors. He blamed these concerns and the loss of the war collectively on the Jews, Communists and other groups. He ignored the fact that each individual person is different. The trauma of blindness on the way to Damascus brought St. Paul to change from evil to good, while blindness brought Adolph Hitler from good to evil. Unknown predisposed thinking may have had much to do with their eventual changes of heart. The Natural Law may have been eating at St. Paul's heart, but passion, outrage and thoughts of revenge were eating at Adolph's. Only God would have a full understanding of these individuals who have had such major divergent affects on world history.

I believe Hitler must pay for his deeds. I believe in justice and restitution of some kind. But no matter how bad he may have been, is a million steel balls of inconceivable pain and suffering going to change all that? Will it ever be justice fulfilled for a miniscule number of years of delirious mistakes? And what is hell? I've been told it is some form of intense physical suffering from fire. Light a match to your finger. How long can you bear it? (Don't try it.) Try to imagine your whole body in this condition for a million steel balls, plus a billion, and more.

I also have been led to believe that hell is the intense anguish of losing the vision of God forever, or that it may be of our choosing. The fear of fire is greater to me than losing God, but only because I have known physical pain, but my vision of God and his infinite love can only be a trifle at this point.

Yes, I fear death. I believe, but I really know nothing. Padre Pio said "do not worry!" This can be comforting. The unknown, however still presents the greatest fear of all. I hope God will forgive me for my lack of faith. I should regret lighting the fire of fear in any reader who heretofore may have been unconcerned beyond his/her daily concerns and joys of living oblivious to such distant realities. Maybe ignorance *is* bliss. Maybe everything will turn out ok. I believe so. Maybe Padre Pio was right.

This fear that many of us share now, points to the destiny or future that will inevitably arrive through the constant progression of time. Death is coming. We cannot escape it. So what can we do about it? Or should we even be concerned? Live and let live, and leave it all in God's hands. He knows what's best. But what we do now may determine in some way the condition of our future.

If so, what we do in the present becomes of enormous importance. This factor must be the governing force for people the world over in what they do today and for the foreseeable future. Most of us may have an overblown sense of self-importance, but, justifiably, we may see clearly that each of us does have a role to play, assuming that our Creator does have a plan; otherwise, why would He create in the first place? Even though each of us is, in fact, a minute element of the Creator's plan, our insignificant awareness can easily place ourselves in a most prominent role within that range of our awareness. The greater our awareness, the smaller the part we see ourselves as playing, but the more accurately would we see.

We have a very limited awareness of what makes up the whole, and we all have an awareness that varies significantly from one person to the next. This limitation invariably keeps that awareness less a part of the whole than we think. The more we realize how much we *don't* know, the smarter we become.

A Christian has his vision; it may work for him. But a Moslem sees a totally different vision; and it works for him. These visions work individually, but in a conglomerate world visions collide.

If an American's aspirations of freedom of the individual leads him to do what is his right as an American, and an Arab's aspirations to follow what he may interpret as the laws of Allah leads him to do what he believes is his duty, what have we got? The clash of right vs. duty ends up in mayhem. This is not what I believe is God's (Allah's) plan, but that of the forces of evil. We have suicidal acts of duty vs. murderous acts of mass destruction, all in the name of service to God (Allah) and country.

Isolating the Arab from the American narrows the visions of each, a trend that is building and growing in today's world towards greater disaster for all of us. There was a time when ignorance was bliss, but expanding communications has brought an isolated world closer together, with its own unavoidable risks. This is not necessarily a bad thing. Eliminating ignorance can only lead to maturity in the long run, if we are ready for it. It is all a part of change, change that *is* a part of God's (Allah's) plan. We have to adapt. We must. Or the forces of evil will win. That is not God's plan, but we all must act to achieve the good, so that some day the good will win out over evil.

Therein lies the one area where unity plays no part, that is, between good and evil. Our world may not be black and white, but the good and the evil in each case must be sorted out and separated, so that we may see clearly to choose both the good over evil and the greater good as well in our complex world.

This picture is very simple, perhaps obvious, but to those of us sheltered by narrow awareness, ignorance if you will, the picture is not so obvious. It translates into fulfillment of aspirations for one at the expense of both.

Fear and ignorance is what led to 911 and other terrorist acts. Narrow exposure and point of view of followers of the likes of Bin Laden led to the horror. The likes of Bin Laden too lack such exposure, just another link in the chain of misguided leadership. When you are blinded by intense passions, consequences of your actions and awareness of the Natural Law of our conscience fade out of sight. The ideals of reason, justice and unity are no longer seen as relevant. The causes that instigate corruption of these ideals may be valid, but the misguided corruption is not.

For those of us who believe that there is a fallen angel of pride and hate, who is the source and director of evil and mayhem in the world, he must be living in seventh heaven (excuse the pun) when division spreads itself everywhere. War and violence never solve anything; they only exacerbate the problem by inflicting pain by one upon the other. Hate, revenge and evil flourishes. Satan wins the battle. Everyone else loses.

We must put an end to all hatred, except hatred for evil. Hatred may be rooted initially in misunderstanding, through ignorance of those hated, who may or may not be guilty of acts of greed, power or other selfish motivation that can only be faced by non-combative resistance. Any attempt to enact violence against the opposition can only result in physical harm to people, innocent or otherwise ignorant of actions taken by their own leaders and representatives. Pinpointing the guilty must be accurate; otherwise, further misunderstanding will follow and the conflict goes on endlessly, involving more and more people. It grows into a continuous exchange of animosities, acted out in hate, violence, tragedy, revenge and war. Do we really need this?

The antidote to this trend is unity. I am not talking about a unity of everyone twisting and superimposing views so that they match. I don't mean the kind of unity where there is agreement on every issue and every detail. The differences still exist. The unity I support is not one of conformity to sameness at all cost, but a unity of all of us in search of truth accompanied by a policy of tolerance with those with whom we disagree. I'm talking about a people unified in a cooperative effort to share views in an attempt to determine solutions to our problems and satisfy the concerns of everyone. The primacy of truth must always be sought and maintained. But, to know or to believe with absolute certainty is a claim that varies from person to person and from one time to another. The need for tolerance, sharing ideas and subsequent understanding is extremely important; unless, of course, you like war and are malevolent toward man.

It amazes me how peace and justice ("liberal" issues) can be incompatible with freedom and independence ("conservative" issues), but that is what a divided world has brought us. It points out the need for working together as opposed to competing and working against one another. When you think about it, peace and justice cannot exist without freedom and independence, and vice versa.

It may not seem possible, but the way our world is diverging, there is little hope for the near future. Either the one side will destroy the other, or the other side will destroy the one. Neither side is perfect. Dominance of one will only result in an imperfect and imbalanced world of one kind or another, no better off than it is now. Maybe total agreement will come someday along with total vision and total knowledge of God's Truth. But we are not now anywhere close to that level of maturity. Perhaps we never will be in this life. Perhaps It is not God's plan for this world.

We are always developing toward becoming what God intends us to be through the spiritual journey each one of us undergoes. That other person may not be ready to advance toward the ideal that we think that we know may be right for that person. But that does not disallow us from planting a seed, or just nudging it along. We may be instruments of the Holy Spirit, but keep an open mind: the Holy Spirit may be at work in the opposite direction.

Any increase in understanding by the one side toward the other, and vice versa, will help create a bed of peace, if only the sides are willing to agree to disagree, and accept the humility necessary for building a foundation of tolerance. This then can lead not to conformity, but to the diversity of understanding, and God's love, the essential message of Christ's visit to God's human creation. Then evil and mayhem can never take over. Satan loses. Everyone else wins.

Occasions, when the rights or customs of one sector of society conflict with the rights or customs of another sector, require working together even more to arrive at a satisfactory agreement. This understandably may not be easy, as the situation in the Middle East has demonstrated. Conflicting religious rights and customs have plagued the area for centuries without solution. Hopefully, some day, the end to violence, much more mutual understanding, a little more openness, a little less stubbornness and a lot more creativity will find a way toward peace in that part of the world.

It has been difficult to break down the subject of unity into well-defined parts, because everything seems to overlap and interrelate. Politics, culture and religion cannot be discussed in isolation without involving each other. World, national or local issues cannot be discussed in isolation without involving each other. Abortion, homosexuality, war, knowledge, technology, etc. in today's world are political, moral, national, international, you name it. The human experience is a mutual blend of all in some form of unity. Where one ends the other one has already begun.

These general topics are vast and complex. I do not begin to boast that I know much about any of them. In fact, who does? In fact, available knowledge of today is miniscule compared to what man may learn during the next one thousand years. In the year 3000 A.D., if man lasts that long, all of his acquired knowledge will be miniscule compared with all that may yet be discovered from there on. Total knowledge may be infinite. I should thereby claim early on that during the course of my life I have never known anything with one hundred percent absolute certainty. I have not *known*, but I have *believed* many things in varying degrees of certainty, but not with one hundred percent absolute certainty. One way that helps me increase my belief in God is by focusing on the extent and complexity of the created Universe. Only a Supreme Being that always existed could put such a physical reality into motion. My loneliness within this vastness leads me to believe and eventually, hopefully, to know someday with one hundred percent certainty. I may want to know Him totally but, I must admit, although I believe with 99 percent certainty, that last one percent, or part thereof, hangs there. It exists due to my ignorance, not my belief or knowledge.

I do not write Unity because I like to write and need a topic to write about, nor do I write Unity because I think I know, or believe, very much about the subject. I write because there is something missing in today's world, and its presence is becoming less and less. Unfortunately, its disappearance is detrimental to a world that should be peaceful and beneficial to man. It, of course, is unity.

I am convinced that disunity is becoming a major crisis. I can see it over and over in two extremes of ideology doing battle, each convinced that he is on the side of the truth, on the side of the good guys, and that, if only everyone could see their way and agree, the world's major problems would somehow go away.

Each one of us can never be exposed to but a very limited number of influences. Those influences have a major role in forming our opinions no matter how independent we may think we are. Those influences all too often are biased in one direction or the other. The sources are usually limited to two: the good guys and the bad guys. Three's a crowd: it confuses the issues. People like things simple: black and white, good and bad. One can choose one side, support everything served up by the chosen side, and everything that goes wrong can be ultimately construed to be the fault of the other. One is spared the awkward chore of having to think. It takes courage for one to move from one side to the other, but that too can result in biased orientation, only different.

A refusal to get together for just discussion purposes with those who maintain an opposing point of view on any issue is a refusal of one's right to express and share one's own point of view. It is a form of disrespect, abuse and failed attempt at superiority over an opponent. It is a relinquishment of that right in a show of inferiority. The ability to grow in understanding of another's state of mind and the chance to develop one's own counterarguments are lost. The one refusing to dialogue, therefore, is a two-time loser and the chance for peace is waived.

The ability to think and respond quickly is not everyone's forte but one can find the opportunity to respond, after careful thought, by writing and sharing, like I am trying to do here.

A prime culprit for the trend toward division is anyone who can benefit or profit from bringing influence to bear on the public's awareness, no matter how shaded, exaggerated, twisted or dishonest that influence may be. No one wants to hear two sides. It is just too confusing. But exposing oneself to the other can only add, not subtract. Agree or not agree, at least one has a better idea about what one is arguing or debating against, giving way to a more intelligent and effective influence.

Another culprit is influence brought to bear on private awareness by political lobbyists. The only difference here is politicians are sometimes financial benefactors of the influence. The public never benefits. They always lose in the long run by unnecessary division and the ignorance that leaves them little more than fools. It is not always that the influence is false, just biased in what is emphasized and what is omitted. No one can know everything, but a balanced vision of what we do know is necessary for the sake of unity.

This problem of divergence and disunity seems, in my limited vision, to be growing, and in every aspect of our lives. It is growing between cultures, between nations, between political parties and ideologies such as in my native country of the United States, and within the realm of religion, the international institution, or, better said, divergent institutions that focus on our future and the fact of our very existence. The refusal to compromise that resulted in the 2013 shutdown of the United States government points out the increasing gap of separation in this world.

Throughout this book I am handicapped by my limited vision of the world through the eyes of an American Catholic, and the reader must keep this in mind. Although a reader from another country or religion may find reference to American and Catholic issues over-emphasized herein, the views I offer as a Catholic American may hopefully provide some understanding of and insight into my religion and country.

DEFINITIONS

A friend once asked me a series of questions that went something like this:

1) Do you believe in killing babies before they are born?
2) Do you believe in giving money away to people who are able to work but don't want to?
3) Do you believe in shutting down the economy by banning use of natural resources in order to preserve all of the land?
4) Do you believe in seeking total equality through equal pay for everyone regardless of work value or quality?

My answers qualified me for status of conservative, according to my friend. So too would most of the people I know who consider themselves liberal?

In like manner one could pose the following series of questions:

1) Do you believe in polluting our air and water so that wealthy corporation leaders may get wealthier?
2) Do you believe in sending our young men out to risk their lives in order to maintain the corporate military complex well fortified financially?

3) Do you believe in giving the wealthy the power they need in order to enslave the poor of the world?

4) Do you believe in selling arms to both nations who are at war against each other?

Or whatever. I'm not sure I am a conservative after all. Conclusion: all liberals are conservative, and all conservatives are liberal. Now that's a sign of unity, don't you think? Obviously, it's all in the definitions we have for our words.

Another friend complained about the world heading in the wrong direction because of Communism and liberalism. I asked for a definition of liberalism. He said: "Liberalism is the act of setting God aside, whereas God should be our focus." That confirms it: I am a conservative.

How we individually define a word is critical to successful communication, pure and simple, not just for "liberal" and "conservative," but for everything. True, it is impossible for one person to have a completely accurate understanding of someone else's word definitions, especially for the meaning of words expressing concepts, usually based on one's lifetime of experiences. These experiences formulate and define our understanding of what words mean. No two people have had the same experiences, so no two people will have the exactly same vision of a word's meaning. Nevertheless, a close mutual agreement on word meanings is critical, at least as close as possible. So some mutual understanding must be established between two people in conversation; otherwise, the two people may go on arguing endlessly and never realize they agree. Conversely, they may think they are in complete agreement, when actually they are not. Too many discussions go on like two ships passing in the night, never having a true meeting of the minds, and the participants never realize it. Webster would be helpful but how often do we have the time to search through the dictionary over every other word of discussion or debate.

One side can find much from the other that is in agreement and vice versa. And many issues are of no great concern one way or other. Why make a big deal about it? Also, it would be wise to establish some grounds for agreement first. This sets up a friendly atmosphere which is always helpful. Then, let's negotiate and resolve the critical conflicting issues.

An accurate understanding of the word unity as I use it in the text of this book is defined in the Introduction. It is critical to understanding my intent. Webster's New International Dictionary, Second Edition, takes 50 lines to define the word unity. The ones that come close to my use are as follows:

"4.b A totality of related parts; a complex or systematic whole" or "5.a A thing that is or seems complete in itself."
Or what may be farthest from my use of the word would be:
"6 . . . . Absence of diversity."

When discussing political, social, and economic as well as religious ideologies, definitions of words are of the utmost importance. Nothing can be more misleading in our understanding of one another than wayward definitions of such concepts. Subjects of these kinds can take on many meanings, varying from one person to another. We all experience these words in a variety of circumstances, and within a variety of contexts, viewpoints, persuasions, etc. Excellent examples would be communism and socialism. Both can be applied to economics, politics and social systems, and a variety of meanings historically. Communism was not the same and for the same intentions during early Christian times, or during the initial Russian approach to counter the previous suffering under the czars or during Stalin's atheistic totalitarian system. Some people see socialism and communism as one and the same, while others may define communism as an extreme form of socialism. One of Webster's definitions of socialism reads: "a stage of society that in Marxist theory is transitional between capitalism and communism and distinguished by unequal distribution of goods and payments to individuals according to their work."

Here in capitalistic and democratic America there are forms of socialism with the likes of unemployment compensation and social security. The communistic Soviet Union did allow for some varying incomes for different occupations.

Before I go any further in exposing my ignorance on these concepts, let's just say that understanding each other's definitions do play an enormously important part in our understanding of each other's views, which in turn is critical towards establishing unity.

When speaking with a non-believer, establishing definitions is also of the utmost importance, but don't expect it to be easy. Like trying to describe the game of baseball to a foreigner to the United States, who knows nothing about the game, it gets complicated. How to describe what a ball and a strike, a foul ball and a home run, or a walk must be described in much detail in relation to how the game is played. These words come easy to one who has grown up with the game, but they mean nothing to the outsider.

In like manner, describing such words as holy, sanctified, blessed, glorious, hail, grace or sacred should be easy, right? Try defining them to an atheist and you may find that you don't fully understand what they mean yourself. Or even the word "love." With such depth and importance of meaning, yet "love" can mean so many different things and with so many shades of understanding, that without a precise definition in its given application, it can be the most misunderstood word in the English language, or any language.

If I use words herein without a clear meaning of intent, I apologize. I will try my best to make myself clear.

CULTURE

The electron is like a planet circling around the nucleus of an atom like the sun of a solar system. Or is it actually: the electron *is* a planet circling around the nucleus of an atom, which *is* a sun of a solar system? Is it possible that there are living human beings, animals, plants or some other forms of life, ever so infinitely small, existing on some of the electrons of some of the atoms?

Our planet is like an electron circling around the nucleus of an atom. Or is it actually: our planet *is* an electron, circling around the sun of our solar system, which *is* a nucleus of an atom? Is it possible that life forms, enormous beyond description, exist up there too?

Is it possible that the atom of our solar system is part of a rock or tree or whatever on a planet that is on an electron of a still larger atom, which in turn is a part of something else even larger yet of a universe so infinitely large that we can never conceive of it from the perspective we have at our scale? And how far does this go on in the opposite direction of smaller scales than ours?

After a hundred levels larger and a hundred levels smaller, then what? Does it ever end? Or am I just dreaming? Let's face it, how do we know? Certainly, we cannot put limits on the creative powers of God. But how can this kind of creation go on forever? So too, how can space go on forever in our own universe before it ends? How does space end? And then, what's on the other side? . . . Mind boggling.

The only explanation as to how can all this end is by taking the largest level of the scales of creation and the smallest level of the scales of creation and make them one and the same, so that we essentially have a physical existence that circles around upon itself in a never ending space warp. In other words, you keep going from level to level in one direction and eventually return to the exact same level from which you started. Impossible? Ask God. Real? Maybe, and maybe not. Only God knows. I am willing to believe that it probably does.

Now, perhaps nearly as mind boggling is the question how does all this relate to the subject of culture? Well, it demonstrates the extent of differences that can conceivably exist in our vast and complex world and the vast array of circumstances and conditions that can form cultures. If you have noticed the vast array of curiosities that have been discovered within our own solar system from planetary explorations, you know what I mean.

In no way can anyone from their very narrow perspective be able to fully understand anyone from any other culture without walking his path, in his shoes, in the same location and at the same time that he has experienced. And that's just right here on the same electron. The possibilities are endless. Many of the physical phenomena discovered in our neighboring planets so far cannot be explained. The only way to begin to understand people from another culture is through dialogue and study. This is important. It means coming together in unity, not standing off from afar and making judgment. We can never fully understand *anyone,* not even those of our immediate families, or ourselves for that matter, but some form of unity can help bring us closer together and thereby discover the greater understanding necessary for loving. As for understanding what exists on other levels of the scales above and below our own, if they exist, we can leave that up to time and eternity. The task of understanding right here on our highly limited electron is enormous enough. For the sake of peace we must expand our awareness to encompass as much of the diversity in this world as we can. To assume everyone can be and should be just like me is extremely arrogant. Arrogance and ignorance go hand in hand.

Africans were dragged over to America from their own cultures and forced into slavery to serve another culture. When freed, they were expected to assimilate into society and adapt to a culture they hardly knew. The only American culture they did know was the extinct plantation life. Blacks could not understand whites and whites could not understand blacks. The melting pot did not include black skin, yet the melt is taking place, but very slowly. Blacks and whites, in the meantime, have served one another as scapegoats for our problems.

What can be said about the Klu Klux Klan? They have their culture too, as divided from the rest of American culture as it may be. Members find the Klan's wayward influences when guidance is needed in their lives, but there doesn't seem to be any. They need to belong. Unfortunate experiences of past rejection and failure create a fertile ground for hate. A convenient pool of scapegoats is provided. Mutual understanding of others goes nowhere, and division grows. Where the desire for understanding is trumped by emotion, there is little hope for peace to grow. How much the origin of the Klan after the Civil War can be contributed to a reaction to the loss of their way of life and the traumas of war, especially Sherman's raid, is not for me to judge. Surely, the actions of the Klan have provided ample cause for judgment.

Love is the one ingredient that can change this. Blacks are likely more open. It may take initiative on their part; risky, but the only way. In time and with patience, walls can be broken down, bridges built, understanding begun and hatred and division dismantled. Impossible? If God is love, how can it be anything but possible? Let's do our part. We can do nothing more. Then, leave the rest to the Almighty.

Jews may have been partially at fault for their isolation, but they never asked for the Holocaust. The Nazis found a perfect pool of scapegoats: successful and isolated. The Jews are God's chosen people, but did they realize they were chosen to lead all the others? Christ's brand of leadership requires service on the part of the leaders . . . In unity. But do we Christians understand Jewish traditions? Do blacks understand the plight of the Klansman in search of meaning in his life? Nobody is perfect.

Cultures are typical examples of how limited influences and experiences create one culture different from another and how peoples of various backgrounds are different. We see it every day, even among families and within marriages. Husband and wife just cannot understand one another. It takes many years to adjust. In fact, it usually takes a lifetime of learning, growing and adjusting, especially in the United States, the melting pot. Some marriages never make it, and fail. We cannot expect him or her to be just like me. The differences can be vast, like they are for experiences and influences. You cannot change the way we're brought up.

Speaking of the melting pot, the United States, or Canada, or any new country that comprises varying cultural backgrounds are wonderful experiments in worldwide unity. Unfortunately, it takes time, a lot of time. Europe is heading in that direction with the influx of people from Africa. In comparison, the U.S. is way ahead of the game.

Peace is a priority for healthy prosperous living. Adjustments are difficult, but, for the sake of peace, they oftentimes are necessary. It is not easy to change, especially if it translates into admission that we have been wrong. The danger still stands, however, that, for the sake of peace, the change may turn out to be from right to wrong.

In summary, a wide variety of conditions mold our cultures as we struggle to adjust and survive, even within cultures and among various life forms. We may not be able to change the conditions, but why would we even want to? Diversity is beautiful. Life would be boring without it.

WAR

Many movies today are so saturated with violence and killing that they have become almost silly. But underlying all the visual mayhem, a sense of insensitivity to it all is slowly replacing an appropriate abhorrence. In each flick there is always the good guys and the bad guys clearly defined, making it a simple task for the viewer to know who to root for. There is no doubt that the villain portrayed is bad. There is never any gray area, always black and white. The unfortunate transition from the imagination of the movie to the reality of life is an easy one: pick a side, our side, the good guys of course.

Choosing our side as good is fine, but the problem arises where this choice always seems to be followed up by the necessity of defining a bad guy, the other side, an enemy, someone to fight against. This kind of mentality eventually leads to the mayhem of our real world.

The silliness of these movies that employ violence as a drawing card to attract ticket buyers is further exemplified, I noticed in some cases, by the incredible accuracy of the good guys' marksmanship shooting down an enemy on every pull of the trigger. This marksmanship is made even more incredible by the fact that the shooters may be in constant rapid motion against an enemy who is moving also, often in an opposite direction. This incredibility is equaled by the enemy's total lack of marksmanship, missing their targets, the good guys, every single time, and perhaps even more incredible by the fact that the numbers of enemies always greatly exceeds that of the heroes: makes the good guys look like the poor underdogs in spite of their incredible marksmanship.

Perhaps even more incredible yet is why do we buy into this kind of stuff. Look at me: how would I know about it if I didn't buy into it myself? Our youth in particular seem to never get enough of it. I might be careless. Or I may accompany some youth to evaluate it after. But I am not a censor. Better to do some research and avoid it in the first place. Every buck spent tells the moviemakers what I like. Supporting these movie attractions is the fact that, with today's advanced technology, they are so well done technically and creatively that what they can do is fascinating in itself. Any treatment of the human condition as it exists in reality is lost. We go to the world of the movies to escape reality. That is ok but not always necessary, and certainly not ok at all cost.

To show violence for what it is, ugly and evil, is much to be admired, but should be to point out the violence and what trouble it causes, not to pinpoint the "bad guys." There is potential good and bad in each and every one of us in varying degrees. The lack of understanding is too often the evil that leads to violence. The simplicity of defining good people as distinct from bad ignores the complexity of the human condition. Documentaries and historically relevant stories do have their place.

Not all moviegoers are going to be affected by what they see. They will see it as just a movie, a form of entertainment, but when the violence is glorified as some flicks are doing today, the violence is translated into good . . . and that is not good. Some individuals may find the visual violence as abhorrent to them. But not everyone is the same. A love for violence that is reflected in the thrill of patriotism, heroism or revenge is emotional and egotistical. Patriotism should be good. Sometimes violence comes with the territory, but not when it requires an enemy in order to be so. Patriotism then no longer has purpose. A true patriot takes pride in providing humanitarian aid where needed. The love of violence as a form of revenge is strictly emotional and usually unproductive by its failure to understand the other party.

I remember the thrill of placing myself in the position of the football or basketball star, with everyone cheering our side on and taking great pride in my heroics. I wanted to be there. The thrill of the ego . . . . In the grand parade down Massachusetts Avenue with my fellow soldiers as the crowds cheer, the president salutes, the love of family and friends and millions of tearful TV viewers. I wanted to be there. We have vanquished the . . . name your enemy or let government find one for you.

Anytime there is unity it should not create sides, one side against another. Unity creates the ultimate goal: oneness, but with diversity in harmony.

A valid question that must be addressed is what to do about the likes of people who have evil aims and will stop at nothing to access to them, at whatever expense—death, suffering, injustice, hunger, poverty—or by whatever means—war, lies, brainwashing, genocide, what have you. Our friend Adolph is one example that always comes to mind.

Neville Chamberlain, prime minister of Britain, tried to negotiate peace with Hitler. It didn't work. I respect Chamberlain's intentions. It was worth the effort if it could have averted World War II, but he didn't know that Hitler could not be trusted.

First of all, in my view, there are two conditions in which war may be justified, and only after all peaceful efforts have been exhausted within a safe time allowed, and justified only for one side, not both, a very questionable and debatable issue as to which side may be justified.

The two conditions that I see justifies war, at last hope and on behalf of one side only, are 1) defense of one's own life or country's existence and 2) defense against genocide. World War II presented both conditions, and only for one side. If a situation presents genocide on the part of both sides of the conflict, then what do you do? Negotiate, negotiate, negotiate . . . . I guess. On second thought, any war can be construed as genocide depending on how you want to define it.

There never was a war in which both sides were justified. For example, in the war between Iraq and Iran in the latter part of the Twentieth Century, military arms were supplied by the U.S. to both sides. "It is in the best interest of the United States," so said Secretary of State George Schultz. He didn't say what those best interests specifically were during the interview I witnessed; but, if best interests they were, those interests must be evil in themselves. War extended or maintained to weaken, demolish, or destroy life because it strengthens one's own strategic interests, is unjustified.

From "Priest for the Third Millennium" Archbishop Timothy M. Dolan writes:

> "On April 28,1997, armed Hutu militiamen in Burundi, forcing all thirty-four resident seminarians to the courtyard in

front of their chapel, where the leader of the invaders demanded that the seminarians divide themselves into Hutu and Tutsi groups. The seminarians refused, huddling together instead of declaring themselves members of any one tribe. Their commandant insisted again, ordering the cutthroats to aim their rifles at the united group of students, threatening to open fire if the men did not obey his command to divide into the two ethnic groups. The seminarians remained united, defiant of the threat. The commandant ordered his men to open fire, mercilessly cutting down in cold blood those thirty-four young Africans, who wanted nothing more in life than to be conformed to the Prince of Peace as his priests.

"... I propose that their martyrdom dramatically instructs us about integrity, as they wanted their exterior stance of fortitude, their claim of fraternity flowing from Christian and priestly identity, and their common desire to love one another even to laying down their lives, to mirror what they believed inside."

Residual evils that rise out of war include prejudicial attitudes of hate toward the other side; such as toward the citizens of Germany and Japan during and after World War II, for Arabs after 911. Despite misguided intentions of many of us citizens around the world, we are all created in the image and likeness of God, born with potential for good. God does not create evil. Man is created good. It is the evil influences that pollute us toward that which is not good and away from God and His plan for each one of us. Narrow influences and experiences can eventually lead us astray. Ignorance and division become the ultimate evils that pave the way for sweeping us into a river of no return if we let it. Understanding and hope pave the way back up that river to the antidote. Love is the antidote. God is love and God is all powerful.

How silly that may sound to some. How sound it may reveal itself if we truly give it a try.

How silly is war? I have been fortunate enough not to have to serve in such mayhem. Those who must experience war firsthand, survival or not, are the best witnesses of what it is like. Survivors may hold onto their patriotic contributions with pride and resent the anti-war demonstrations that appear to downgrade their sacrifices. They *should* feel justified for their pride in their sacrifices for the reasons they hold dear, but they need not overlook the abhorrence to war by demonstrators. The two may do well by sitting down together over a cold beer and sharing a mutual understanding. With passions set aside, they may find they agree on more than they think . . . . Unity.

James Michener wrote a book called "Poland," based on historical facts. Assuming his research to be valid, reading this book became both exhausting and frightening from the endless injustices imposed on the Polish people by marauding bands on horseback that raced from village to village, pillaging, killing and raping. How could these offenders be so cruel and selfish? Little in the way of governmental security existed in some areas centuries ago. Perhaps immature youths came under the influence of the pleasures and excitement offered by such groups, never giving a second thought to the suffering they caused by joining in. Only selfish interests maintained their focus. But didn't the Natural Law ever rise into their consciences? Dialogue as an option was never offered and the poor defenseless people did not have the means to fight back.

The causes of conflict may be valid, but resolution of the conflict by war is the greatest human folly of all time. And its horror continues to worsen.

I know a women who claims to be an atheist. How one can know without question that a God does not exist is beyond me. Agnostic maybe. The influence of her father, also an atheist, was strong in her life. He fought in World War II, and afterwards would no longer believe that a God could allow the horror that he witnessed. If I saw what he saw, could *I* believe in a loving God? Who am I to judge, having not witnessed what he did, and not by his choosing? His experience: just a cup of horror out of the ocean of wars that have contaminated human history. This could be one bit of evidence that there may be some form of sadistic intelligence, an adversary of God, behind what generates evil in the world. If there is a God, there may also be the absence of a God.

The people of Japan, Germany and Italy are our friends today. We buy their cars. We visit their countries. They visit ours. It seems impossible today that we hated them during World War II. What's the difference? It wasn't the people as much as the leadership and the propaganda they spewed that drew the people into war. There had been suffering in Germany due to unmerciful punishment imposed upon them because of World War I, but it took charismatic leadership to exploit the hardship into revenge and the horror of another war. Hitler eliminated the possibility of dialogue, understanding and unity and replaced them with the creation of enemies.

In the upper St. Lawrence River, between the province of Ontario and the state of New York, during the War of 1812, on Christmas Eve, soldiers of opposing forces curtailed their preoccupation of the day and joined together in the middle of the frozen river to celebrate their mutual holiday. They partied, sang songs and returned to their posts. A day later the stupidity of their duties recommenced. Loyalty to duty overrode loyalty to the heart. For what? Leadership cannot find agreement, so a worse horror ensues. Today, nearby towns on opposite sides of the river memorialize the war from each of their own limited points of view. The unity was lacking in 1812. The unity is lacking today.

"The War," produced by documentary filmmaker Ken Burns, is not a movie that inspires patriotism and war in a harmonious blend. Comments like no World War II soldier could stand more than 240 days of battle without going mad, yet most would not last that long without being killed or wounded, and Japanese soldiers on Iwo Jima were ordered to kill as many Americans as they could until they too were killed, do little to glorify the violence. One man who was interviewed said "I survived, got married and lived a happy life, while many soldiers left their blood in the sands of Iwo Jima. I could have been one of them. Why was I so lucky?" That man rides on a wave of undue guilt over the fate of his companions in battle.

The Old Testament can attest to this belligerent habit of man. Even God himself led the Chosen People of Israel to mass mayhem in protection over adversaries, a documented fact that I have yet to comprehend. Like the atheist, I do not understand. Were their adversaries all bad guys? It is hard to understand this aspect of His divine plan. Maybe I am failing to understand the pulse of those primitive times. I am not one to judge God, nor is anyone else. The Christian version of an all merciful and loving God seems so much more acceptable to me.

Albert Einstein is well noted for his genius at advancing the knowledge of science, but not everyone is aware of his insight into world affairs and the causes of war. In "Einstein on Peace," a compilation of letters and speeches on the subject of war, edited by Otto Nathan and Heinz Norden, published in 1968 and 1981, is a voluminous work of 640 pages covering from 1914 until his death in 1955. A few samples of his views are as follows:

In an address to a Franco-German demonstration organized by the German Peace Congress in Berlin in July, 1922: "I believe the condition in which the world finds itself today makes it not only a matter of idealism but one of dire necessity to create unity and intellectual cooperation among nations." p. 51.

In an interview with George Sylvester Viereck of New York in 1931: "The masses are never militaristic until their minds are poisoned by propaganda . . . . Our schoolbooks glorify war and conceal its horrors. They indoctrinate our children with hatred. I would teach peace rather than war, love rather than hate." p.125-6. A Jew preaching Christ's message of love. Our faiths are much more alike than we think.

In a speech at the University of Southern California in February of 1932: "Disarmament and security cannot be separated; they must come about simultaneously. Security will be achieved only when all nations commit themselves to abide by the decisions of an international authority." p. 164.

In a 1931 article in the New York Times: ". . . the greatest obstacle to international order is the monstrously exaggerated spirit of nationalism that goes by the appealing but misused name of patriotism." p. 152.

In a letter to Sigmund Freud in July of 1932: ". . . political power hunger is often supported by the activities of . . . that small but determined group, active in every nation, composed of individuals who, indifferent to social conditions and restraints, regard warfare, the manufacture and sale of arms, simply as an occasion to advance their personal interest and enlarge their personal authority." p. 189. So little has changed.

Einstein strongly supported the acts of concerned peace supporters in resisting conscription and any participation in the violence and killing of war. But in the 1930's Hitler and Mussolini gained power. Despite considerable criticism, he was forced to change his position as indicated in a letter in August of 1933 to one of his critics: "So long as Germany persists in rearming and systematically indoctrinating its citizens in preparation for a war of revenge, the nations of Western Europe depend, unfortunately, on military defense . . . ."

"I take little pleasure in saying this, for in my heart I loathe violence and militarism as much as ever; but I cannot shut my eyes to realities." p. 230. He was so prophetic, it is sad to say.

POLITICS

Two of the most popular political satirists today are Rush Limbaugh and Michael Moore. Two of a kind, right? Yes, they are. If they have a comment to make, it will never be in recognition of anything valid from the opposition. Please excuse me if I am mistaken. They both may have important views to be considered, they both do it with humor, and you always know whether it's going to be a conservative view or a liberal view before they ever say a word. Enjoy the humor, but check both sides before making a commitment. If you love the humor on one side only, I need say nothing more about the tragic division that exists in this country. The chasm of division they are spreading is not helpful. The same goes for serious commentators on radio these days. Let us encourage debate, not misleading single mindedness that rarely offers the total picture.

Rush Limbaugh once told his millions of viewers on TV that Chelsea Clinton was ugly. Do you want your 14-year-old daughter cast as ugly in the minds of millions? Michael Moore pursued Charlton Heston at his private home to make a point in his movie about the NRA. He knew very well that Heston was suffering from Alzheimer's Disease. Was this necessary? If you listened to either and found it funny, did you think about the individual hurt underlying these actions? I find both repulsive. Such actions call for apologies by both parties. Frankly, I find Chelsea really cute. When it comes to finding solutions to controversial issues, satire seldom provides incentive for progress.

Today, the one side never listens to the other, only ignores. There is, however, one group in our nation that actually does listen to the opposition. That is, surprisingly enough, the politicians. They are the ones who must nail policies into laws that must be written into the books. Without compromise nothing ever gets done. They are *expected* to get things done. No politician that gets nothing done can expect any support and adulation, whether it's making legislation or blocking it. The problem they face is the other side, who are always there, and must be recognized or they may block their cause. Convince them, compromise, give and take, whatever, but one must listen. They cannot be ignored. Tolerance has nothing to do with it. It's accepting what they are reluctantly willing to in order to gain what they truly believe in. It's a bit of expediency on all sides. But, when it is election time, compromise and give and take are left behind on the campaign trail.

The simplest and most basic political definitions of the words conservative and liberal are: conservative means stay the same and liberal means change. Both conservatives and liberals play important roles: to improve current conditions requires change (liberal) and to prevent worsening current conditions requires prevention of change (conservative). Determining which is the right solution in a given proposal, improve or worsen, is the chore of those in control to work together towards a solution. But, unfortunately, you can't please everyone.

Even when we consider such hot issues as abortion, failure to understand each other's concerns (liberal and conservative) stands in the way in finding viable solutions. Must it always be a matter of good guys and bad guys? The immediate reaction to opposing views is to set up a wall of rejection and anger that creates division, and prevents even the hope of increased understanding of the other side as well as growth of God's truth that may be absent in our own awareness. Ignoring concerns of the other side does not help.

Sitting down with the enemy, although difficult, may be the first and only possible step towards finding a compatible conclusion, if that's possible. I believe, that with tolerant and compassionate, rather than combative and emotional, minds, much understanding can be achieved of God's truth. The widening expanse of division is the devil's playground.

Division is a basic ingredient for evil and misery. Satan glories in the gravy of our division. Satan grows to fill that expanding chasm with confusion, hatred and misunderstanding. Those who do not believe in a devil may substitute the word evil in its place and still get my point.

Exploring new and different forms of thought should always be acceptable, even encouraged. That is the only way we move along the road toward a better world, and, more importantly, toward preparing ourselves for and adapting to a changing world. But we must always follow that road with a mature and cautious attitude, so that inroads to what is good, beneficial and right can be separated from what is not. Hence, there is a place for both conservative and liberal thought, but there should be no place for division, festering animosity and the failure of the two fields of thought to penetrate one another and blend into the best and most workable solutions to problematic issues. Such solutions should be the best of both worlds, not a watered down version of the two.

If one side doesn't learn what the other side has to say, how is it going to argue intelligently their side against the opposition about which it knows nothing. The problem is the one side is not interested in arguing (debating) with the other side in the first place. They are the enemy. Which points out the fact that division reigns, not unity.

It is necessary to address all issues and concerns of the opposition, not just those one has pat arguments for, while ignoring the ones that are more challenging and present the danger of thinking a different line or confusing the chosen agenda, or, worst of all, requiring the potential admission of having been wrong.

From my limited perspective, political division in the United States began to grow wider back in the 1960's, 1970's and 1980's when concerned liberals began to uncover questionable policies of injustice toward Third World countries by multinational corporations, along with, of course, disagreements over the Vietnam War. Unrest at that time was as much against the Johnson Administration as it was the Nixon Administration. Anti-American feelings were openly expressed in spite of a vast population of loyal patriotic Americans who were sensitive to such rhetoric against their beliefs. The liberals showed little sympathy for conservative sensitivities, in spite of their love for the history and good faith of their country's past. So conservatives, in turn, ignored legitimate liberal concerns and sought a defensive response to unpatriotic activities. Liberals wanted to make their country right. Conservatives wanted to preserve what is right about America. The two sides split further when they could have come together to resolve legitimate differences. In stead, enemies were created. The heat was fueled, as usual, by politicians wanting to get reelected.

The division has grown ever since, feeding other issues: for example, environmental concerns became a liberal issue, and economic concerns became a conservative issue. Should the cost of gasoline skyrocket, or should the ecosystem be sacrificed. Exaggerations on both sides have been prevalent. What do we do? Choose a side?

In a unified effort, the best and most balanced policies could resolve the conflicts in the best interests of all concerned and all citizens in general. With tongue in cheek, we should beware of the danger that policies do not wind up adopting the worst of both sides, ending up with everything bad and nothing good. Is that possible? I hope not.

Politics have become so exposed to the people, thanks to the growth of media technology, that it affected everyone's thinking through the politicians' need for electoral victory. Everything becomes black and white: we have all the right answers while the others are demonized in the public's eye. Both the Democrats and the Republicans in U.S. politics are *both* black and white, if you listen to both. At least that's what the voter is faced with. Choose who you want to believe. Fortunately, there are independent thinkers who actually do the electing. Unfortunately, their choices are severely restricted by party agendas, plus they are handicapped by exaggerations, lies and ignorance. No one has a grasp on the future except God. Politicians can only have a limited affect.

Our political leaders and candidates must reveal both the benefits and the consequences of their proposals and policies, not just the benefits alone. The consequences will be revealed by their critics unless they risk exposing themselves to their own shortcomings. Too often the voices of critics are never addressed by their targets, leaving the independently discerning public with the responsibility of figuring out what is true themselves. Not addressing criticism then only leads to greater ignorance and confusion.

I would recommend establishing requirements by which leaders, writers, corporations, politicians, etc. may establish the facts regarding a particular issue to resolve intelligently their differences. This would be particularly useful in the case of extremists and those with widely divergent views. The two sides must meet frequently and periodically to discuss the facts along with proofs and sources of their evidence. Let these meetings continue, with sensible breaks, until they both agree on all counts. No agreement, no discontinuation of the meetings. Sooner or later the facts will be established if participants ever hope to discontinue the meetings. The one side will be a fare judge of the other and vise versa, and the pressure of admitting the truth is on both sides if they wish to avoid the meetings from continuing forever. The drawback is the risk of the meetings never ending. Nothing *would* ever get done. In this case, extremists could go on meeting while moderates could make necessary temporary decisions.

In addition, it is interesting to contemplate another requirement that each side of an issue write their version of the opposition's views and then exchange results to show evidence that all sides of an issue is adequately understood before continuing. Hard copy beats verbalizing any day for complete understanding. It would take a lot of time, but wouldn't it be worth it?

The two primary political parties in the United States have traditional platforms that may serve as guidelines for its members, but it becomes inflexible when these guidelines become requirements for candidates. Dennis Kucinich of Ohio was actually pro-life but turned to a pro-choice platform in order to run for president as a Democrat. This type of policy creates the situation of the party controlling the individual candidate, rather than the candidate given the opportunity to set policy for the party. The voter too is given an inflexible choice where he cannot vote in presidential primaries for a candidate in stead of the traditional party line.

Now I have alienated both liberals and conservatives. Thanks for reading my book. Have I set myself up as universal scapegoat? It would be worth the sacrifice to bring this world closer together. The moderates in the middle don't care. Then again, the moderates too will make noise when someone in their family is selected by lottery for the "The Hunger Games."

I recently attended a movie showing at a local Catholic Church, one that is quite conservative. The hall was filled from one end to the other with interested parishioners and friends. The movie was a highly political production and the showing was followed by a talk by a local politician running for office. The purpose of the documentary was to demonize every aspect of liberal politics. One example that struck me the most was regarding environmental issues. There was nothing positive mentioned about efforts toward environmental preservation. The environmental movement, needless to say, is a liberal one, or at least so recognized by some. The movie indicated that the movement is run by communists. The audience loved it. It was all about what they wanted to hear. All one-sided, even to the point of distortion. I asked the pastor afterward whether or not he felt the movie was one-sided. He said he believed in presenting both sides of the issues. I agreed. I don't know when the liberal side was or will be presented, but, so far, I regretfully have missed it. Some Hollywood movies shown in their hall, however, have shown flexibility.

In 2012 a movie called "The Hunger Games," in which the laws of a fictitious country required that two representatives from each territory be selected and forced to roam about an area in search of meetings with each other for competitive battle to the death to determine one individual winner. The reps were selected by lottery. Lucky them. The theory is that these games would absorb all other citizens' human nature towards war, and the kind of revolution that occurred 75 years earlier, and was suppressed by the government. The guilt and blame aspect would be channeled through these games, thereby, like Christ, the lottery victims became sacrificial lambs, absorbing all the offenses of the rest of the people and allowing them to go on with their daily lives by fear and distraction away from any cause toward physical war that would involve everybody and threaten the government's power and control. (One exception here would be Christ's choice to be sacrificed, not by lottery, but by prophecy and the will of the Father.) I am not sure how successful the movie's approach would be. In the end, an ironic turn of events changed the people's acceptance of this practice, that is evil in itself, not because it brought peace to the land, but because of the continuing injustice. Majority rule does have its flaws. A valid point that it does bring out is the human desire to find a scapegoat to blame for all that's wrong with the world, without searching introspectively to ourselves for possible guilt: a rare approach for many of us, let's face it. In the case of the state of the world today, this scapegoat conveniently arises in the side not chosen by each one of us.

Ron Dzwankowski, in his column for Sunday's Detroit Free Press, May 20, 2012, writes:

> "These political and social scientists [including Brendan Nyhan, assistant professor of government at Dartmouth College, and others] have concluded that once people have made up their minds about something, showing them abundant evidence that they are wrong prompts them not to change their minds, but to dig in their heals and seek affirmation outside the reality-based world . . . .

". . . People today don't challenge their thinking with exposure to new or different ideas; in stead, they seek information that reinforces what they believe. They do so with either little knowledge of the source or blind trust, both of which are dangerous.

"This is not exactly a scenario for progress. I don't know how we're supposed to move forward together if we can't find any common ground.

"But how do we fix this? How do we get to a sensible middle ground where I think most Americans—not the noisiest ones— would like their leaders to be, so politics can be about public service instead of seizing power?

"'We need trustworthy people outside the partisan realm . . . people who care about their own reputations for accuracy and honesty,' Nyhan said."

In a follow-up e-mail to Ron, I said "You hit the nail on the head."

THE ENVIRONMENT

Another major issue of the day is the environment. It too divides conservatives and liberals and serves their political platforms with corresponding agenda. Protecting the air, water, ozone layer, etc. is actually conservative in nature: you know, conservation. The problem lies in the fact that this costs money, and creating the products we use every day must be controlled in order to best provide for environmental protection. Now we are into the world of business. So, the conservative political agenda has set their priorities with business: the economy takes precedence. And, to follow the pattern, liberals take their anti-business positions by condemning the deplorable wreckage of our environment by producers of products we all use.

In the liberals behalf I must add that their pro-environment agenda has been in place for a considerably long time. It seems only more recently that conservatives have jumped on their own bandwagon to try to disprove all that the liberals have been claiming. Yet, no issue has been setting up division more than those surrounding the environment, and no issue could better be served by mutual unification. Business is the core and the environment serves up to it on the political scene.

Let's begin with changing weather patterns. There has been a significant warming trend for many years. One cannot deny statistics. Temperatures are higher. Glaciers are melting. Whoa! Who says they are? Not the conservatives. There are glaciers that are growing on the other side of the

North Pole. True: about 4, according to the recent documentary "Chasing Ice." But this is miniscule to the number of those that are melting, and at a momentous rate, as the movie clearly indicates. It's just a cyclical warming trend, says the conservative agenda. But records indicate the warming trend is off the chart as compared to scientific evidence of previous cycles, says "Chasing Ice." Shall we just argue about causes while we wait and see?

No matter what is causing the trend, if we don't do something, disaster is on its way. During the last cycle, if that's all this is, there was no millions of people living along the lowland shores of New York City, Boston, London and wherever around the world. Those four expanding glaciers may be a savior for Alaska, Siberia and the arctic shores of Russia, but what's going to save Los Angeles, Tokyo and Hong Kong? Flooding may not happen overnight, but eventually hundreds of millions of people may become environmental refugees, or at least cyclical refugees. The question is not the political one, who or what to blame. But the practical one, what are we going to do? If it is cyclical, when does the cycle reverse gears? Do we know? And what if the conservatives are wrong? Whoops! Oh well, to err is human. If somebody has the answer as to when this warming cycle is over, please step forward! We need to know. We need to be prepared. We could go a long way toward finding a solution, if there is one, by getting together, than by fighting over it. Did I say that business is at the core of environmental issues? I take that back. Getting your vote at the next election is the real core.

No one wants to breath smelly air or drink contaminated water. Correcting our mistakes of the past will cost money and restrict our manufacturing. Both will have an affect on everyone. The core of the division between conservatives and liberals, other than politics and money, is to what degree does it become undesirable. No one will complain about kicking up a little dust into the air but all will object to the release of killer nuclear radiation to ravage its effects on our health. The question that really divides us lies in the degree. To what extent does pollution affect us before we should do something to control our lifestyle? Somewhere between kicking up the dust and a nuclear holocaust, obviously. But where? That question divides us. Working together, searching for the facts, regardless of politics, may generate sensible solutions.

Should we care about the polar bears? Is our lifestyle more important than a polar bear's life? Or the survival of its species? Becoming an environmental/cyclical refugee may not be of great concern to folks living inland until refugees start crowding into their areas looking for residences, food and jobs. Drowning is probably equally traumatic to a polar bear as it is to me, regardless of their level of sophistication on the order of Creation. The loss of such awesome creatures to extinction would be very depressing to most of us.

The potential of the endless variety of plants in serving man in his effort to cure disease is becoming more realized every day. Yet, species of plants are simultaneously going extinct every day. The race goes on: preservation and cure versus extinction and disease. How much can we afford to lose? Preservation of land specifically allotted to farming may be an issue whose time has come, or is long overdue. Environmental consequences affecting northern Africa are already in progress, causing immense hardship to its people, who must migrate for their survival.

How do we turn these developments around? Is it possible? Or do we let nature take its course and not worry about it? There is something to be said about laissez-faire. Too many times man's attempts to correct one problem leads to more problems worse than what they are intended to correct due to ignorance. Can we ever, or will we ever, do the right thing?

It is true that Nature does recover and correct itself, if we let it. This wonderful quality can only occur if we stop the preventive policies that caused the problem in the first place.

There is one form of environmental destruction that leads all others in the degree of its devastation: that is the nuclear holocaust and the radiation resulting from it. There is no known effort on the part of man that can reverse such pollution. It is said that Nature will correct such contamination, but it will take 4 million years. That is a little longer than my lifespan, or anyone else's I know. Perhaps this is the Purgatory that we as Catholics believe we must enter into to pay for our sins before entering into the joy of God's presence in eternity. Unlikely. As far as the planet is concerned, there could be some species that can survive nuclear radiation and continue to propagate and begin the process of evolution all over again. Hopefully, they would become smarter than any species that would cause a nuclear holocaust: perhaps maggots, or black flies, or starfish. It would take a long time.

FOOD

Without a doubt, food is an issue that affects us all.

I have never liked the idea of eating a living thinking creature whose life has been sacrificed for my benefit. But many of God's creatures sacrifice other creatures for their survival, and that's all a part of Nature. The system evolved, I assume, according to God's plan. "Why" is a question I will pose when I face the Creator in eternity. I will present it with respect, of course, and without trying to be critical. After all, I eat meat, and I have no right to be hypocritical.

The Old Testament indicates God requested that lambs, goats and doves be sacrificed for forgiveness of sins. And I'm sure Jesus ate fish. Meat is one of our best sources of protein, which is necessary in anyone's diet. I respect Hindus who, for religious reasons, refrain from eating animals. Yet Hindus I have known do not impose their diet on others. Being vegetarian is a difficult habit to carry out. I'll just leave it at that. There are other issues that relate to food.

According to an article by Mackenzie Hall, R.D., in the March 21, 2013, issue of the Detroit News: "The organic industry is . . . The fastest growing sector of the supermarket."

One of the controversies floating about today is whether organics are worth the extra cost. If you're poor, less is more when it comes to cost. The short run must take precedent over the long for many of us. For some, organic is a minor luxury, but well worth it for concerns of health, according to those who support it. This issue tends to divide the conservative versus the liberal format as well: liberals believe in and support organic and conservatives see it as a money-making gimmick. Most people, the moderates, don't know who to believe. But business is intricately involved in the controversy. Unity then is an unlikely incentive if money is the core value on the part of producers, whether it be organic or not. If one can afford the moderate extra cost, organic is not going to do any harm and, if poverty prevents it, non-organic is not going to hinder immediate survival.

I suggest that, because organics are something new, it must be liberal, and what we have been used to over the years is the standard acceptable way, and therefore conservative. Nonetheless, it wasn't too long ago that the food producers began adopting organic methods, something new. Most people never knew about it until liberals found that acceptable was not so.

According to Mackenzie Hall, "a study released from Stanford University . . . concluded that there isn't much difference between organic and conventional foods." Mackenzie Hall goes on to mention other studies that counter the Stanford study. Believe whatever suits the agenda of your chosen side, or be honest and admit you're as confused as I am.

Chemicals that are used for fertilizers (growth hormones, pesticides, preservatives, coloring, flavoring, or whatever) does bring into question the potential harm to health in the long term. To avoid questionable farming practices in what we eat, Alyson Mitchell, Ph.D., of the University of California, Davis, suggests a practical approach, such as selecting organic fruits "with thin skin, like strawberries and grapes" and conventional fruits "with a thick peel such as oranges or bananas."

Where big business generates greater production, honesty can be left by the roadside. Ads that boast their product as organic are oftentimes no better than anything else, so claims some non-profit organizations who support organic foods. Government labeling regulations may be weakened by loopholes. Big business found them; then the critics did too.

By taking an overall nonpartisan view of the issue, it becomes evident that the seriousness of how the food that we eat is, like environmental issues, a matter of degree. Most people are concerned about anything that they believe may do harm to their health, particularly anyone who has experienced health problems. And that includes just about everybody, but here again we are talking about the degree of problems. No one wants to be sick again, once they know what it is like. The ignorance and doubt that most of us are subject to regarding food leaves us in a quandary, not only for the food and how it may be produced, but whether or not to take medication versus healthy food as a source of treatment. We all seem to fall prey to the latest storyline we have heard on how we should govern the food that we eat. At least, I must admit, I do: what I heard yesterday replaces what I heard a year ago, which has become no longer relevant, in my current awareness, at least for now.

The Detroit News article also mentions a project by the Rodale Institute that takes us back to the subject of environment: "The project found that organic farming uses 45 percent less energy, 40 percent less greenhouse gas emissions, and better supports soil organic matter compared to conventional systems."

Looking further into the subject of food, we find that eating is an activity of pleasure. We eat when we celebrate. We sacrifice it during Lent. It gives us a feeling of fulfillment. But, above all, it tastes good. Matters of health, personal appearance, the sacrifice of fellow creatures and monetary cost all give way to the pleasure of taste when it comes to food.

Another issue, already touched on in the chapter on the environment, is farmland management. A unified and honest study, free of politics, of the relative land efficiency and production, including cost, of the mega farm versus the traditional more intensively worked small farm is greatly needed. Which is best? Or, is there a place for both? Opinions diverge. Big business claims the mega farm is necessary for supplying the world's needs. After all, is there enough organic fertilizer out there to supply the world's vast need for food? Those who favor smaller independently owned farms claim theirs provide more efficient use of the land. Survival of their family's operations are at stake. Meanwhile, government support has favored the mega farm in the past. Maybe there is a need for both to complement one another, in a *unified* effort.

Now we come to the only food-related subject whose importance outstrips all the rest: hunger, or, in the extreme case, starvation. Hardly anyone can look at a photo of a child wasting away from starvation without wanting to feed him on the spot if one could. I have no reason to doubt the claims charitable organizations make calling our attention to the tragic conditions that exist in many parts of the world, mostly in northern Africa right now, due to changes in environmental conditions or war. We are lucky not to be among them. Many people are compassionate. They want to do something to relieve the suffering and the death, and they do. World starvation has been reduced some in recent years, but it still exists.

I worked with a young man who recalled a time when he had no money except the salary he was paid at the end of each month. He said his biggest fear was the last couple days before payday when he might run out of food and money. Just a couple days without food posed suffering that was intolerable. I cannot doubt him. I have never had to go without food for as much as 24 hours. How long does it take to starve to death? How much suffering does starvation entail?

No issue should call for our attention more than people who are starving. Anyone exploiting this issue for personal gain would be the lowest form of humanity, if that. Besides changing environmental conditions and war, starvation can result from political struggles, genocide and just poor distribution of the world's goods. There are many charities that address this issue, but, so far, in spite of all the good they do, it is a long way from saving every last human being from starvation.

Unity again plays an indispensable part by focusing the world's awareness more intensely on starvation and what we can do to eradicate the horror. All charities working together may eliminate some duplication, and thereby extend the benefits further. Such coordination can yield the benefits of the best methods. Also, charities can maintain their individuality, yet increase production through a combination of mutual support and friendly competition.

ECONOMICS

Let's begin by describing the extremes of political opinion regarding the distribution of and rights to money.

At one end is the liberal condemnation of Capitalism as the ultimate cause of greed and exploitation of the poor. Communism is the answer to the call for equal rights of all citizens for a piece of the financial pie. Sounds simple and fair. But did the founding fathers of the Soviet State anticipate the waning of incentive that comes with blocking the desire to get ahead and earn funds that would enable one to satisfy passions to attain more expensive things, passions that the next person may not share?

At the other end is the conservative condemnation of Socialism and the welfare state as the ultimate destruction of freedom. Laissez-faire is the answer, the call to guard against restrictions that inhibit citizens from their right to compete for as much of the financial pie as they wish. Do we realize the innate temptation for greed to take over, after more modest goals have been reached?

Wall-mart has been criticized for setting up shop on the outer edge of small towns and using their massive financial corporate support to undersell established local stores and put them out of business, and then raising prices to their standard levels, still much lower than the prices of the stores in town they replaced. This is obviously unfair practice. Most people don't care: it's money saved in their pockets.

Some will argue that defunct store owners were gouging their patrons anyway and living in the elite part of town. Wall-mart is only doing what the other corporate chains have been doing. They have to compete. It's a sign of the times: the age of small family owned stores is in the past. Wall-mart provides jobs for the community (including something for the unemployed former entrepreneurs) and many products that are now affordable to poor families (including former entrepreneurs). They may include basic necessities that they could never afford from established locally owned stores in the past. These arguments seem hard to contest.

At the other end of the chain, and the reason why Wall-mart can afford to provide inexpensive products, is the exploitation of Third World families who are hired to make and farm the products for Wall-mart. These stories are horror stories I've been hearing about families with children who must work along with their parents long hours seven days a week for wages that barely enable them to feed themselves. Is this an exaggeration? What are the facts?

Exposure of these evils have embarrassed the likes of Wall-mart and other corporations, but are they being corrected? Or are they just exaggerations? Just exaggerations according to those who benefit from the reduced prices, and that includes most of us. These companies know where the money is coming from, and where it is going. Simple economics tells us that income is a good thing and outgo is bad. You please those who bring it in. You give as little as necessary to those who take it away. It's good business practices. But is it good Christianity? . . . Or Judaism? . . . Or Islam? . . . Or Buddhism? . . . Or the like.

Surely, enslaving families in El Salvador cannot be justified for the sake of more clothes for kids in America. Meanwhile, the truth of these arguments gets battered around between the liberal and conservative agenda. With a concerted effort on the part of both sides, the truth could be established, but we, unfortunately, are too preoccupied with battering it around on behalf of our chosen sides.

There doesn't seem to be any plausible solution to this conflict, even if all sides get together in good faith, but something could come out of it that would be fair and livable. Let Wall-mart sell its wares to satisfy the common everyday needs we all share, both rich and poor: food, clothes, soap, tooth paste, etc. Can local entrepreneurs concentrate on specialty items that Wall-mart doesn't handle? With Wall-mart's size, it can easily afford to provide counsel to local entrepreneurs on how and with what products the two can complement one another's offerings of merchandise and not compete. This would require considerable adjustment on the part of small businesses, but with Wall-mart expertise some form of compromise can be reached. Wall-mart could hold back on selling certain products just to make everyone happy. This way Wall-mart can provide its presence, local people can benefit from lower prices and local entrepreneurs can stay in business.

I use Wall-mart here only as an example. I could use the others interchangeably. But what if there is more than one chain in the area? How do we get Target and K-mart, for example, to work along side the others in town? Now the situation gets more complex. Such a plan is easier said than done. With a unifying effort, perhaps under the guidance of the local Chamber of Commerce, who knows local conditions better than multi-chains, some compatible directions and policies could be established.

Let's get it together! But is that enough? If we just put our heads together, will we necessarily find solutions that will lead to fairness and happiness for everyone? No. Can it be an improvement on today's situation? Yes, but everyone may have to sacrifice a little. The poor of America may have to sacrifice a little with slightly higher prices in order to benefit any horror experienced by their brothers in Third World countries. And corporate CEO's must do their part. Would a spartan salary of eight million dollars a year be too much to bear in lieu of ten? And then there are the professional athletes: need I say more? There must be other means to satisfy their egos besides money. How much do we need?

As for world poverty, it is out-of-sight, out-of-mind, and out-of-mind, the sky's the limit! When the eyes see only green, the sorrows of poverty and need are off the screen. This is Capitalism run amuck. The solution to preventing Socialism and a welfare state is curbing greed.

This brings us to jobs. Jobs are what enables patrons to make purchases that keep the manufacturers and distributors in business, who hire people to do the jobs that keep the products coming, and round and round it goes for any healthy economy to exist. Not long ago, our manufacturers had the brilliant idea of avoiding high wages by closing plants in the north and opening them up in the south where wages were lower; then, for the same reason, on to Mexico; and then to foreign lands where wages were trivial compared to union controlled wages back home. One manufacturer started it and, in order to compete, others followed. Now they could build their products for less and compete with the competition. Citizens of the Third World obtained badly needed jobs and were happy to work for little in economies that demanded little to survive. One thing they often could not afford were the products they were making. The automobile would be a prime example, along with all the parts.

Meanwhile, back in the states, a ten-year recession is under way. Ten years! Unheard of in modern day America. Even the Great Depression didn't last that long. Whose going to buy the cars? Eliminating jobs on the home front left a giant gap in the number of traditional car buyers. What caused the recession for the automobile industry is a no-brainer. The same goes for other industries.

Overseas jobs versus jobs at home. Both are needed. What is the solution? I don't know. Slower transitions might help. But how do you control economic dynamics? How do you see into the future to know what's coming before it's too late?

Another major contributor to our ten-year recession was the intended gift by our legislators of housing to poor families so that a home could be had for a low mortgage payment. Nice idea in its intent, but what about adequate procedures and controls? When droves of buyers are unable to pay the low mortgages, homes get repossessed, properties flood the market, values plummet and the banks need bailouts from the federal government to survive. Did anyone see that coming? Does anyone benefit? We need the banks, but did they get bailed out from need or did they benefit? I cannot answer that. I need the facts. It may vary from one bank to another. Our legislators seem to have demonstrated a lack of foresight unequaled in American political history. A piece of guidance was missing in the final plan that was adopted and approved.

These issues cannot be resolved easily. My insight and expertise into economics and marketing is as trivial as wages in Third World countries. But what seems obvious to me is the need for some form of togetherness in working out our problems, and mutual understanding of them. Competition is good when it forces manufacturers to provide a better product. That is what Japanese car manufacturers did to GM, Ford and Chrysler. But the drawbacks exist, and can lead to serious problems detrimental to society. Where do we draw the line? Maybe that's where government must do its part. Together. Both liberals and conservatives, with their corresponding ideas and reservations.

Unions played a major part in expanding buying power of workers hired to do necessary jobs, both skilled and unskilled. The unskilled today are being nosed out of the picture by automation. They never saw it coming. With many years left before retirement, their jobs no longer exist. Education and skills are the wave of the future. We all must be ready: the new entries into the job market as well as those in the position to train potential workers. The young trainees and workers of today must also realize that any particular skill may not provide the security of a lifelong job. Flexibility is becoming a part of life. These factors must be reflected in union policy.

Unions at one time were strong, good for individual security, but they may have been cutting off too large a section of the economic pie. Their jobs may have been boring and grueling and deserving of a substantial wage, but union power may have gone too far for some of the demands on behalf of poorly educated workers.

But now conservative political forces are pushing too far in the opposite direction. Unions are important. Without effective unions, some trades may find themselves being used and lost in poverty due to a shift of power that favors greed by another powerbroker. Without mutual understanding, justice for all can never be realized.

Obtaining an adequate job these days, adequate for survival by U.S. standards, requires an education. Pumping out hamburgers for Burger King may attain a lucrative wage for dependants living at home, but for a family bread winner, who must pay for food, heat, living quarters and transportation, that high school diploma is a must. And to enjoy a little more that higher education is becoming the next necessary step.

For the woman who drops out of high school to get married, has children, then loses her husband through the unexpected trauma of death, divorce or deportation, is stuck with the impossible task of survival. Dependence on a bread winner is no longer an option. Living off the streets is unacceptable with children, especially where winter weather is not friendly. Most jobs today confront the job seeker with application online only. Computer literacy has become the latest impossible task confronting the poor. Attempts to gain access to welfare are complicated by the same frustrations that websites provide, like answers to only the obvious questions and no human to talk to about specifics.

Sometimes I believe that the computer has become the great invention that allows us the easy way to get rid of poor people who don't count. Besides, computers cost money, and access to the local library requires local residency. So much for those lazy dependents on the welfare state, not that they don't exist, but what percentage of the unemployed population do they make up will vary, not according to the facts, but according to what side of that issue one has chosen to support.

HELL

I have thought many times about what is the difference between those who make it to heaven and those who go to hell. Every single human being is a complex of opinions, habits, beliefs, influences, reactions, works and so on and so on. Which ones make it? And which go somewhere else? Is it all really fair? Or are we all cut and dry, black and white, good and bad? There are those who have sinned exceedingly and never regretted it and, at the same time, done wonderfully good things to benefit the common good. Will the person who satisfies his/her sexual passions by cheating on his or her spouse, but creates beautiful music, art, architecture or whatever to be enjoyed and uplifted by man throughout the ages, be condemned? Do they not contribute to God's plan in spite of their transgressions? Will we be judged on the good that we do, or don't do, or on the bad that we do, or don't do?

Christ said: "He who believes and is baptized shall be saved, but he who doesn't believe shall be condemned." Mark 16:16. More than anything, I want to believe, but sometimes doubt creeps in. Where does that put me? Is there a little bit of a doubting Thomas in each one of us? Or don't we dare?

There was a movie that won an Academy Award for Best Picture in 2005 called "Crash." It very beautifully demonstrated how there is both good and bad in each one of us. Is not the saintly person being sinful when criticizing someone else for their sin when only God knows or understands the full nature of the sinner. "He that answers before he hears shows himself to be a fool, and worthy of confusion." Proverbs 18:13. ". . . he separates them one from another, as the shepherd separates the sheep from the goats; . . . these will go into everlasting punishment, but the just into everlasting life." Matthew 25:32,46. Jesus clearly indicates the differences between sheep and goats as to what they did to the least of his brethren. (The entire passage is included in the next chapter.)

One may ask for a definition of the least of Christ's brethren. This is a legitimate question, and an important one. He did not go into details, leaving it up to individual interpretation, unfortunately. But for the scope of this book, I would take the liberty to define it as any human being that we may meet in the course of our lives, from the most important and powerful down to the least important and least powerful, with special emphasis on the latter, as implied by the word "least." They obviously would stand as the least likely ones who may draw our attention. I might extend that to include anyone who may *seem* to be the least likely to need our care or interest. You never know what may be boiling inside the lives of total strangers no matter what our perceptions might be. I might further extend that definition to include non-human creatures of the animal kingdom. What could be more least than them? And how far down the animal chain should we go in this category, a subject that takes us out of the scope of our focus?

In any case, we all have done some good sometimes and bad other times to the least of God's creation. So what creates the essential differences between the goats and the sheep? In other words, what constitutes the dividing line between going to heaven and going to hell? Can one good deed win salvation? Or is that not enough? Does the multitude of bad deeds outweigh that one, or outweigh the smaller number of good ones? These are simple questions, but very important ones if our eternity depends upon them. Even the characters from early history in the Old Testament committed sins of sexual indiscretion and deception. They seem, at times, to contribute to the continuation of God's plan, including people in the line of Christ's ancestry.

As I speak of unity here on earth, it will eventually lead to the ultimate unity of the knowledge of God's goodness, truth and love in eternity. Hopefully, all will be unified then. No exceptions. No one in an eternal hell. Even Satan will hopefully recognize his mistake. He must be subject to the element of time. He was created the angel Lucifer, then at some point in time decided he should not be below his creator and master. If he can reject God, then why not repent? So that all truly can become one . . . . Not for me to say. Evil is evil, the absence of good. Evil can never be unified with the goodness, truth and love of God. However it will be, it will be the fulfillment of God's plan.

As for the existence of some highly intelligent fallen angel known as Satan, I refer you to the Wedding Feast at Cana section of the chapter on the Rosary for additional thoughts.

I quote Fr. Ron Rolheiser: "Hell is the absence of something, namely, living inside of the life that's offered to us . . . . Hell, as John Shea once said, is never a surprise waiting for a happy person, it's the full-flowering of a life that rejects love, forgiveness and community." ("Rolheiser's Reflections" on page 6 of the Michigan Catholic, October 30, 2009.) A good example of this is Ebenezer Scrooge in Charles Dickens' The Christmas Carol. He lived in a temporary hell on earth until he finally came around. An interesting concept, and believable. He goes on: ". . . as we get older, a deeper kind of loneliness can and should begin to obsess us. This deeper loneliness makes us aware how torn and divided is our world and everything and everyone in it. There is a global loneliness that dwarfs private pain . . . . We live in a world deeply, deeply divided." ("Rolheiser's Reflections" on page 6 of the Michigan Catholic, February 13, 2009.)

I wonder if heaven will be better appreciated after experience in the difficulties of life and any Purgatory that may follow. Can the joy of heaven and God's love be greater with knowledge of pain and a so-called "hell on earth"? The moment after suffering? Does knowing suffering make heaven any better or genuine than if we never suffered? Have the angels ever experienced pain and suffering and the ups and downs like we do in life?

Let's face it, life is not easy. But is it necessary? Would we be any different if we went right to the prize and skipped the pain? Must the prize be earned? Interesting thought. The way we are is to be prone to sin. God creates us as imperfect beings, dependent on each other, and marked by Original Sin according to my Catholic teaching. The angels' story must have been a test as well, if some of them are fallen angels and some are not. I am now getting into territory beyond my awareness, so let us go no further.

The joy of a soldier and his family, after survival of his ordeal and return home from the battlefield, can never be known in the same way by those who are spared the trauma. His new freedom can only be appreciated all the more having known its absence. But the memory of the horror lives on. He must live with it the rest of his life. Is it good or bad? For the dead, it is another story.

In 1846 the Donner party of pioneers heading for California got caught up in early winter snows over the mountain pass, now named after them. Is knowing the joy of survival after the trauma going to make their lives any better with the memory of 39 lost family and friends whose corpses served the other 48 with the only means of sustenance for their four months of freezing horror? We will know all the answers to this and many other questions, but not until after our heavenly prize is finally realized.

Another interesting question: Can we be happy in heaven, if someone we knew and loved in life didn't make it, and is not there with whom to share the joy? Is that possible? If God is love, how far does love extend? How can God's love be limited? He may even love those in hell because that was their choice in life, but what about those in heaven who loved those now in hell? Is their joy abbreviated? Or is their memories blotted out and ignorance is their bliss? I find this difficult to accept.

JUSTIFICATION

Justification: actually, I never heard of the word used in relation to salvation. Now I'm finding out that it is the initial issue that created the division between Catholicism and Protestantism. "Justification is seen by Protestants as the theological fault line that divides Catholics during the Protestant Reformation." (comment on July 21, 2009, by syntyche, Roman Catholic Resources website.) Justification is what makes a sinner righteous before God and by which he reaches salvation. It is essential to self-preservation and how we will spend our existence for eternity. What can be more important than that?

Simply put, Catholics believe that we are saved by both faith and good works, while Protestants believe that we are saved by faith alone, but the Protestant view varies with differing shades of meaning from one religion to the next. Another side of the same coin is that one is saved at the moment when he/she accepts Jesus Christ as our savior. It is then a done deal. Salvation is secured. Catholics believe it is an ongoing process that takes a lifetime of doing good, based on faith. It is never done until death's departure.

Someone is going to accuse me of following the line of my Catholic background, but so be it. It sounds like the Protestant version would be really neat: do whatever you please and there'll be no guilt, no restitution. Does this mean I can rape, murder, abort, cheat, steal, hate, perform all sorts of sordid sexual acts, etc. today and, as long I have faith in Jesus as my savior, all will be heavenly tomorrow. Anything and everything goes; I am saved. Maybe that's where our friend Adolph stood on this issue. Meanwhile, the sincere God-fearing Jew, who would not accept Jesus Christ as his savior because he remained loyal to the faith of his parents and religious leaders, and has suffered imprisonment, painful medical experiments, starvation and a horrible death, will be subject to eternal damnation. And, of course, the Nazis who inflicted this horror on him can be eternally happy. Maybe I have been seriously led astray by my Catholic upbringing, but I have always thought that our Creator was a just God. Protestants should be able to correct me on any misconceptions I might have.

Let us take a brief look on the variety of views of justification among Christian religions according to Wikipedia, the free encyclopedia on the internet:

Anglican/Episcopal: "The subjective aspect is faith. trust in the divine factor, acceptance of divine mercy. Apart from the subjective aspect there is no justification."

Methodism: "We are accounted righteous before God only for the merit of our Lord and Saviour Jesus Christ, by faith, and not for our own works or deservings . . . . we are justified by faith alone . . . if one fails to persevere in faith . . . justification may be lost."

Eastern Orthodoxy: "The Eastern church sees humanity as inheriting the disease of sin from Adam, but not his guilt; hence, there is no need in Eastern theology for any forensic justification. Justification is a living, dynamic day-to-day reality for the one who follows Christ."

Lutheranism: "Lutherans believe that individuals receive this gift of salvation through faith alone."

Reformed: "John Calvin's understanding of justification was in substantial agreement with Martin Luther's. Calvin expanded this understanding by emphasizing that justification is a part of one's union with Christ."

Catholicism: "In Catholic theology, all are born in a state of original sin, meaning that both the guilt and sin nature of Adam are inherited by all . . . . As the individual then progresses in his Christian life, he continues to receive God's grace both directly through the Holy Spirit as well as through the sacraments . . . . At the final judgment, the individual's works will then be evaluated."

If you wish, you may check Wikipedia for more detailed descriptions, but, for me, the more detail doesn't clarify these summaries any more conclusively than these brief extractions. Excuse me for my shallowness.

Translation from two different passages from three bibles may point out more clearly where some confusion may exist. Yes, where; but the question of who is right and who is wrong is another issue; one I am unqualified to answer. If I had expertise in the original languages of Scripture, I may be equipped to come up with my own translation, unqualified as it may stay still be. The following are these two passages, starting with John 1: 29:

"He <u>alone</u> is the Lamb of God who takes away the sins of the world." From Martin Luther's Smalcald Articles.

"'There is the Lamb of God' he [John the Baptist] said 'who takes away the sin of the world.'" The Oxford Study Bible.

"'Behold the lamb of God, who takes away the sin of the world!'" The New Catholic Edition of the Holy Bible.

Note Martin Luther's word <u>alone</u> (my underline), which does not appear in the other two versions.

And Romans 3:23-24:

"All have sinned and are justified freely <u>without their own works and merits,</u> by His grace through the redemption that is in Christ Jesus, in His blood." From Martin Luther's Smalcald Articles.

"For all alike have sinned, and are deprived of the divine glory; and all are justified by God's free grace <u>alone,</u> through his act of liberation in the person of Christ Jesus." The Oxford Study Bible.

". . . as all have sinned and have need of the glory of God. They are justified freely by his grace through the redemption which is in Christ Jesus." The New Catholic Edition of the Holy Bible.

Note again the missing portions. One must then ask the question: were the missing portions deleted from the intent of the original writers, or were these same portions added to the intent of the original writers? It seems that it wouldn't take an insurmountable effort for experts of various faiths to sit down together and determine objectively those intentions from the earliest texts that we have available to us.

In 1999 the Joint Declaration of the Doctrine of Justification was signed by the Roman Catholic Church and the Lutheran World Federation, stating "consensus in basic truths of the doctrine of justification exists between Lutherans and Catholics . . . . we confess together that good works—a Christian life lined in faith, hope and love—follow justification and are its fruits," Not all Lutherans and Catholics agreed to this signing, leading to further disunity within, among their respective constituents, but hopefully it will be a step forward towards a common ground.

Roman Catholics point to the passage of Matthew 25:31-46 regarding the final judgment, which is very much essential to justification, when Christ said:

"'When the Son of Man comes in his glory and all the angels with him, he will sit on his glorious throne, with all the nations gathered before him. He will separate people into two groups, as a shepherd separates the sheep from the goats; he will place the sheep on his right hand and the goats on his left. Then the king will say to those on his right, "You have my father's blessing; come, take possession of the kingdom that has been ready for you since the world was made. For when I was hungry, you gave me food; when thirsty, you gave me drink; when I was a stranger, you took me into your home; when naked, you clothed me; when I was ill, you came to my help; when I was in prison, you visited me." Then the righteous will reply, "Lord, when was it that we saw you hungry and fed you, or thirsty and gave you drink, a stranger and took you home, or naked and clothed you? When did we see you ill or in prison, and come to visit you?" And the king will answer, "Truly I tell you: anything you did for one of my brothers here, however insignificant, you did for me." Then he will say to those on his left, "A curse is on you; go from my sight to the eternal fire that is ready for the devil and his angels. For when I was hungry, you gave me nothing to eat; when thirsty nothing to drink; when I was a stranger, you did not welcome me; when I was naked, you did not clothe me; when I was ill and in prison, you did not come to my help." And they in their turn will reply, "Lord, when was it when we saw you hungry or thirsty or a stranger or naked or ill or in prison, and did nothing for you?" And he will answer, "Truly I tell you: anything you failed to do for one of these, however insignificant, you failed to do for me." And they will go away to eternal punishment, but the righteous will enter eternal life.'" The Oxford Study Bible.

There is no mention here of faith at all to determine one's justification for being either a sheep or a goat.

At the beginning of the Sermon on the Mount the beatitudes (Matthew 5:3-10) laud attitudes or characteristics that clearly imply good works, such as "those who show mercy" and "peacemakers." Other passages include:

Matthew 7:21, John 5:29, Ecclesiasticus 7:32-36, Ezekiel 18:1-9, among others.

For any effort toward the goal of unity, we must clarify our beliefs regarding all the above passages by establishing definitions of such words as faith and works. Then we can more effectively debate the subject of justification, or any subject for that matter. Two debaters who unknowingly define their terms in their own minds differently will never make any progress. This happens quite frequently.

Certainly, some guidelines are very important for all of us to follow on our path towards God's love and salvation, but I might add a question to the doctrine of justification: whose place is it to justify who is saved or who is not? Catholics? Lutherans? Or whose? Maybe it's God's place, not ours. Theories on justification can be strictly for guidance, nothing more.

One thought that has always rested in the back of my mind is the self-interest of our actions and goals throughout life. In other words, how worthy or righteous are we really in setting long term goals for ourselves versus the short term. Are those of us who live in service to God through our works and sacrifice as altruistic and righteous as we think we are? Or are we just that much wiser in goal seeking as we seek the eternal reward as opposed to something here and now and temporary? How devoted are we to just serving God, versus how devoted are we to that promise of heavenly benefit? Either way, self-interest may lie at the heart of our actions whether temporary or eternal.

It seems to me that God is fully aware of this characteristic of our nature. That's the way He created us. Isn't rewarding actions directed towards long lasting ends a self-interested goal for those who are wise enough? How much does wisdom come from God-gifted intelligence? How much from the blessings of influences that lead us toward heaven? This may have some reflection on the parable of the Prodigal Son. Not all of us are so gifted with intelligence and proper influences. This is where God's mercy and death of redemption on the cross plays full measure of taking away our individual efforts and replacing them with Salvation by God's infinite Mercy. All we need is faith, as some Protestant religions maintain. The primacy of faith. Again, however, keep in mind that, if we truly have faith, we do good works as a necessary bi-product. With faith we cannot *not* want to do good works in service of our Creator, either in service of our long term goals, or perhaps out of some inner altruistic need for showing gratitude for all that God has given to us. It is an interesting question.

Those who have made the wise choices in life are also given greater responsibility for what we do and are expected to do more. There is no reason for the highly devoted Christian to look down upon seemingly bad people. No one can fully understand the intentions, the opportunities, the sincerity and the complexity of all the elements that form a person's character. We can and should help guide one another. Such efforts are needed, as they become a part of a person's influences, but only God knows all and only He can judge.

One Catholic belief is that of Purgatory, a form of punishment or adjustment. It seems impossible for everyone, in a single lifetime, to grow in maturity and understanding of God's infinite truth and love to be able to absorb, or even begin to absorb, the nature of God. Does not some further development of our own nature and attitudes lie necessary in order for us to experience what God is all about, the Infinite? For people who have lived average lives but are unprepared at death for their heavenly reward, but not so bad as to deserve eternal damnation, Purgatory may be that form of final preparation. It may consist of experiences that enable us to understand the evil of our sins committed during life; why they are evil and how they may hurt others by being hurt ourselves. The punishment fits the crime. Hindus may call it reincarnation, another life that leads us to understand the same thing. In the long run, it is God's infinite mercy that is in control to bring us to Him, prepared for His Truth.

In summary, the concepts of sola fide, or faith alone, and faith plus good works need to be seen in a somewhat different light. Faith, yes; faith in a higher order, no matter what that might be, above our natural bent toward "me," and me above all others, and toward a realization that what is best for the common good is also what is best for me. That is what Christ's message was all about. Without faith in that higher order, there is little incentive to do good works that lead to the common good. But, good works are a necessary result of faith and a sign that one does believe in the saving grace of Jesus' redemptive act. Anyone who does nothing good and says he has faith is fooling himself or is lying. Good works are the fruits of faith by their very nature.

BIRTH CONTROL

"Abortions are very common. In fact, more than one out of three women in the U.S. have an abortion by the time they are 45 years old." Planned Parenthood website.

There is one thing I fail to understand: if you support life, you are against peace and justice, and, if you support peace and justice, you are against life. Of course, it is much more complicated than that, but in general terms, as they are being used today, it seems to hold true. And that brings us to one of the most divisive topics of the day: abortion. I happen to support peace, justice *and* life. If that offends anybody, you may as well take this book back to the store and get your money back, because you're not going to like what I say, and I can't help you.

The peace and justice movement is essentially a liberal thing, The pro-life movement is essentially a conservative thing, bringing abortion, an intense moral issue, into the political arena.

I must establish the fact, from the very start, that the human fetus is a unique human being, and not just a blob. Even pro-choice people I know will not deny that. It is a medical fact that every bit of DNA in the physical make-up of the future born human is already there right at the moment of conception. To me, that says a lot. If the fetus is left to nature and allowed to develop, it will in time escape the confines of the womb into the world: a human being, unless, of course, some intrusive and unnatural means of violence is enacted upon it.

I don't think partial birth abortion needs to be gone into here. There is never any justification for such a procedure. If you haven't returned this book by this time, it may not please you that anyone who supports extraction of half of the ready-to-be-born human being and crushes the brain, and calls it legal because the other half of the body is not yet out of the mother's womb, is, in fact, sick.

Because I am a Catholic, I have been accused of sticking to the line of the teachings of the Catholic Church on abortion. I do not deny Catholic influence, but irregardless, am I immune to logic and common sense? I don't think so.

The Catholic Church has been criticized for its stubborn condemnation of abortion by the public, and its repeated references from the pulpit by Catholics who believe that peace and justice issues have been vastly neglected. I agree that peace and justice issues are not emphasized enough, especially from more conservative priests. But abortion issues are too often neglected by liberal priests, like a taboo. In fact the seriousness of the issue could very well warrant greater treatment from conservative priests as well. Unfortunately, the pulpit allows for just so much time, while many other valid issues scream for attention. Also, controversial issues alienate the congregation. You can't please everyone. Alienated parishioners will leave for more compatible parishes, thereby deepening division.

There are many problems people face in life, real problems, serious problems, that lead them to seek solutions, one of which may be abortion. One may wish to put off raising children until later, so that they may pursue a career, an education or other such laudable goals. Or due to poverty, a family seems to be impossible. Or the fetus may be subnormal, and would be faced with very difficult problems for himself and the parents. In some countries the sex may be undesirable because only a male can fully contribute to the welfare of the family in their culture. Being caught with an unwanted pregnancy may be a source of great embarrassment or parental consequences. The list goes on and on. The bottom line in these situations comes down to this: priorities.

What is more important? A human life or an education? A human life or the financial means to raise a child? A human life or the fear of embarrassment or strict parents? Once again, the list goes on and on. Invariably, the priority always comes down to a human life. In every case, the only choice whose consequences are certain is abortion. There is one case, however, where the consequences of carrying the fetus to its birth almost justifies abortion as a solution: rape.

One can argue that carrying a child for nine months whose DNA is one-half that of a man who defiled you selfishly and violently is justification and good cause to abort. This argument is hard to deny. The problem is that that unique human being is not responsible for his/her father's actions. The blame rests solely on the father, not in any way on the fate of the fetus. If allowed to develop, it will be born. In no way, is it justice for that potential child to pay the price of the father's weakness. Again, the priority: human life. Admittedly, I may not fully understand all the trauma and hardship and pain, both physical and psychological, that the potential mother is faced with. Yet, does anyone fully understand what it is like to be aborted, nor what is denied the child in the absence of a lifetime? What is done is done.

The father, on the other hand, may often have gotten off scot-free, but with increased knowledge of DNA today, the likelihood of a rapist paying for his crime is great. That man must pay, and pay, and pay. He too has serious problems that must be addressed, but he must be held responsible.

Is carrying this child to birth going to find any valuable compensation outside the offender's willingness and ability to make restitution? The fact that it is a child of God, who will be born with one-half the mother's DNA, going to help? Will the possibility of adoption going to help? It is a tragedy for both the mother and the child, and it should prove equally tragic for the father, not out of hate or revenge, but out of what justice is possible for the mother and child. What is beneficial for the father is what psychological and spiritual help he may be able to get, and need.

So what about the question on contraception? Artificial means of preventing conception have been developed to guard against unwanted pregnancy, without abstaining from sex and suffering the physical, psychological and moral risks of abortion, but Christian churches have condemned contraception in varying degrees, depending on the denomination, another area of disunity. The Catholic church, in particular, has been among the most outspoken as well as strict.

To begin with, their are health risks. Supporters of President Obama's mandate supporting birth control "say it's about health, not religion." But, according to an article by Jeanet M. Kemmeren in the July 21, 2001, issue of the British Medical Journal, among others "The side-effects of the pill include . . . cervical cancer." But according to Planned Parenthood's website, "Today, we have many safe and effective birth control methods available to us." But, according to their section on teen pregnancy, "Women who abstain until their 20's . . . are less likely to become infertile or develop cervical cancer." If their birth control methods are safe, what would cause the cancer? Just having sex? I don't get it.

But what about morality? If the pill clearly affects only the prevention of male and female sperm from joining together to create conception, then why is contraception condemned by the Catholic Church? No human fetus? No problem. In many years past, the only purpose for sex was having children. No children? No sex. This narrow view begged for further considerations, including couples who are unable to conceive because of physical defects or age.

In 1930 finally, Pope Pius XI's encyclical Casti Connubii stated: ". . . any use whatsoever of matrimony exercised in such a way that the act deliberately frustrated in its natural power to generate life is an offense against the law of God and of nature, . . ." but ". . . in matrimony as well as in the use of the matrimonial rights there are also secondary ends, such as mutual aid, the cultivating of mutual love, and the quieting of concupiscence which husband and wife are not forbidden to consider so long as they are subordinated to the primary end and so long as the intrinsic nature of the act is preserved."

In 1994 Pope John Paul II added: ". . . when there is a reason not to procreate, this choice is permissible and may even be necessary. However, there remains the duty of carrying it out with criteria and methods that respect the total truth of the marital act in its unitive and procreative dimension, as wisely regulated by nature itself in its biological rhythms." Complicating the issue with various shades of meaning (read all of Casti Connubii, John Paul's statement, in addition to Pope Paul VI's Humanae Vitae), makes it all too much to decipher for a necessary application by the common everyday married couple who may be getting it on late one evening. An accurate application may require a legal specialist that they cannot afford for proper interpretation. Plus, how many people have ever taken the time to read them? How consistent are the interpretations of priests, the most convenient source of advice on religious matters? The rhythm method, so I've been told, doesn't always work anyway. No wonder these guidelines are being ignored. Viagra is on some health insurance plans for men, so why not contraception for women? According to the U.S. Conference of Catholic Bishops website, Viagra *corrects* a medical condition causing infertility, which is unnatural. Contraception, on the other hand, *causes* the unnatural result. There is a difference here between health insurance and benefit.

Since various Christian churches have stated a variety of positions on the morality of contraception, disunity among them stands as a powerful block towards unity because agreement on this important issue would require rescinding on previous positions. Admitting that one is wrong, or even flexible, can lead to awkward and humbling reversals that may result in an image of weakness and loss of trust. It is too bad because these differences are, in many cases, not significant.

The freedom of choice for the potential mother came into being legally in 1973 with the Rowe vs. Wade decision. It was brought into popularity by the liberal movement along with longing for peace and justice throughout the world, which for so long took a back seat to priorities of greed and power and breakdowns of cultural, political and religious understanding.

Accompanying the goal of free sex came the denial of the responsibility of consequences. In the 60's a whole knew world of freedom broke through, and lay subject to problems; problems that found its solution in contraception and, if need be, abortion. The custom of marriage has been an accepted practice for as far back as recorded history may go. The young of the 1960's, resting on their clear insight regarding the evils of war and injustice in the world, extended their confidence one step too far. Marriage has existed, not as a silly and unnecessary pre-sexual ritual, but for sound, practical, long-proven reasons, something the youth of the 1960's overlooked.

One obvious way to avoid pregnancy outside of marriage is a very simple one: don't do it. But that too carries with it injustice of a different kind. Anyone wishing to raise children but lacking the natural ingredients to attract, or just never had the good fortune to meet the right person, lacks the other partner necessary for complete child rearing. Or one may be stuck with the misfortune of dire poverty that prevents any reasonable hope of raising a family in the near future. But their is always hope. Again: priorities. You don't marry, you don't have sex, you don't get pregnant, etc . . . . Well, that's obvious to most of us. It's a tough life. Sometimes injustice plays a role in our lives.

The stance most conservatives have on abortion is clear. The stance most liberals have is murky at best. It is my suspicion that many liberals side strongly with the movement toward peace and justice but refuse to contend with pro-choice liberals because of comfort in compatibility with constituents. Again, the choose-a-side syndrome draws one into an excuse from the courage of exorcizing any independent thought in order to fit in with the group.

Pro-choice Catholics I know do not believe in abortion per se, but they feel they should not impose their religious moral beliefs on everyone else. Can this be a copout in order to feel comfortable with their pro-choice liberal constituents? Abortion is a legal right that must be protected according to those who believe it to be so. Let us look at it this way. Murder of any human already born into the world is also a very serious moral issue. Murder is illegal and merits severe legal consequences. What is so significant about the natural transition from fetus to child? The child is no longer dependent physically on the body of the mother, but dependent on the mother in new ways every bit as important, and vulnerable to certain demise if abandoned. Tell me, what's the difference? Am I implying that abortion is murder and should be punishable as a crime like any other murder? The answer is simple: yes.

It is generally known that many women who have had an abortion experience problems of guilt and depression the rest of their lives. It never goes away. The decision, in hindsight, may not seem as necessary as it once seemed. A human life. Gone. It cannot ever be retrieved. There is no going back. There is no undo button to cover this mistake. You wonder what he/she would have been like.

I will not go into all the health risks during and following the abortion procedure. An honest physician can describe them better than I.

One definition I want to establish here is soul. What is the soul? Webster's New International Dictionary, Second Edition, takes 102 lines of description to define the word soul. For those interested, refer to Webster. Books have been written on this definition alone, but for simplicity's sake I would define soul as a sense of consciousness or awareness, established by God in each one of us at some point in time, most likely at conception. Although we have no memory of being in the womb, the fetus is very much alive and growing. Where else would God create the soul? We do not know for sure, but can anyone prove one way or the other? The fetus seems aware enough to know when it wants out, kicking away when near birth. And when, during the continuous progression between conception and birth, would seem a more likely point to mark the birth of the soul than at conception?

If the human soul is actually created at birth or somewhere in between conception and birth, my point of view, as well as that of most religions, on abortion merits reconsideration. Since no one really knows, assuming it to be at conception appears the only safe way to go. Who are we to tell God when He is creating each person's soul? We still, nevertheless, are faced with all the physical and other characteristics of DNA that are created at conception.

Life is enough not to define the soul. Plants have life, but without any self-awareness, at least as far as we know. Maybe they *do*: no one I know ever claimed to have been a plant to verify such a claim. They do respond to soft classical music, so I'm told. Maybe plants *do* have souls. I'll leave that up to God and plants.

What about animals? Surely, more sophisticated ones have indicated without doubt that they are fully aware of things. What about less sophisticated ones, like an ant? Is it just a mobile plant or rock, without consciousness? If I place my finger in an ants path, it will run off in the opposite direction, fully aware of the potential danger that confronts it. Hence, an ant has a soul, at least according to my definition . . . . I think I am getting off the topic. Animals and plants are taking us totally into another subject beyond my intent for this chapter.

If there is life after we die, what happens to the fetus that never had the chance of life? Like murder, the victim is deprived unnecessarily of the balance of what could have been anything, but no one will ever know. To the woman who faces this lifelong trauma of having had an abortion, I would suggest the following: make your peace with God. Wrong was done, and forgiveness is a part of God's mercy. No, no one can go back. What is done is done. But admission of guilt and God's forgiveness can ease the pain. The fetus, in whatever state, cannot be anywhere but wrapped in God's glory. That fetus will not hate its potential mother. Their is no place for hate in heaven. What this means to the potential mother as far as restitution and payment for the crime is concerned, is another story. Be grateful for the opportunity.

HOMOSEXUALITY

This is another moral issue that has exploded into the political arena, because of the proposed legalizing of gay marriage. The political conflict over the measure boils down to financial benefits to married couples, more so than anything else. Do we spend tax dollars on a benefit that involves what is believed to be immoral behavior by many citizens, if not a majority? What sexual behavior is performed privately does not have any affect on anyone but those who perform it. Many people find it disgusting and unnatural; but is it unnatural to the homosexual? Obviously not. To them, heterosexual behavior may seem unnatural. But what is it in the eyes of God?

One important key here is a part of the answer to the question: are homosexuals born as such or is their orientation learned due to influences? Opinions vary. It is possible that adverse experiences may turn some individuals against sexual desire toward the opposite sex, developing sexual orientation toward their own sex out of anger or response to rejection, or just a fulfillment of something gnawingly absent in one's life. Or perhaps one makes a choice based on affection received by the same sex early in life before full exposure to sexual development has a chance to lead one into a more normal experience. Somewhere along the line a choice is made. Or is it a choice? One homosexual once commented that: "Why would anyone want to be a homosexual?" Yet, he is one, apparently through no choice of his own.

To my knowledge there have been no or few studies conducted to ascertain insight into what determines sexual orientation. I'm not sure anyone really understands homosexuality and its causes, not even the homosexuals themselves. I'm not talking about studying the performance of homosexual activity itself. This doesn't seem to be of any benefit. I'm talking about interviews with homosexuals to find common threads of influence in their past and present lives that may point to discovering why and how; and of course whether they have been born or influenced toward this condition. Such a study would be lacking in popularity by heterosexuals not burdened by the condition or have self-conscious or adverse feelings about it, as well as homosexuals who may feel self-conscious or uncomfortable about providing any input that may seem an infringement on their personal privacy. It was recently brought to my attention that studies have been done on the brains of homosexuals through autopsies. Some distinguishing physical factors common to them showed up, which indicate the condition may be a result from birth. But can the brain develop these factors through specific activities during life? We have much to learn. Quite frankly, without further data, I have no clue and little to offer.

The important benefit of such research is that, if the condition is learned or chosen, and not by birth, measures can be taken to prevent the condition from replacing what Nature intended. Without the necessary knowledge, we have no idea what to do.

I once suggested to someone who is considered an authority on homosexuality that a gay man and a lesbian woman might find attraction to one another, but I was assured that "it doesn't work that way." This seems to indicate that the orientation may be physical and/or emotional.

On a moral or religious basis, I have been told that homosexuality can be compared to alcoholism as a genetic condition that is not the norm, nor is it the fault of the individual prone to this activity, but as long as it is not practiced, it is no sin. That is the approach suggested by most Christian churches. This kind of pronouncement is easy to make if you are heterosexual and not faced with a future of denying yourself of any deep intimate relationship that brings the kind of fulfillment that, as a heterosexual, you may enjoy. It can bring loneliness and depression for many. If it is God's creative will to mark a minority of us as homosexuals, it is an indication of severe injustice, but you can say the same thing about any condition that plagues someone or other, whether it be a chronic disease, a handicap, a lack of intelligence or any other condition. No one is immune to problems in life. Nonetheless, alcoholism can be controlled just by not taking a drink, but the desire or need for intimacy hangs over the psyche of the homosexual, without just denying oneself of a drink. It can gnaw away day in and day out for a lifetime.

So I ask once again: what is it in the eyes of God? Searching through Scripture for some clue finds the Old Testament stating: "You shall not lie with a male as with a woman; such a thing is an abomination." (Leviticus 18:22) and "If a man lies with a male as with a woman, both of them shall be put to death for their abominable deed; they have forfeited their lives." (Leviticus 20:13). The same fate is prescribed for blasphemers (Leviticus 24:16). The method of capital punishment for the blasphemer is prescribed as stoning. Who is responsible for carrying out such laws? I would turn a deaf ear to any information on acts of blasphemy or homosexual activity. I don't want to know about it. Should I obey these laws in some states in America, I may find myself on the electric chair for carrying out such punishment. So much for the Fifth Commandment.

No one I know atones for their sins as prescribed in Leviticus. If we all atoned for our sins as indicated throughout the book of Leviticus, sheep, goats and doves would soon become extinct or their breeders would be immensely wealthy.

Let's face it: the laws of Leviticus are not very popular these days. Either you follow all of Leviticus or none of it. It doesn't make sense to pick and choose what is to your liking or safety from consequences. "Do not think that I have come to destroy the Law or the Prophets. I have not come to destroy, but to fulfill." (Matthew 5:17) Christ fulfilled the laws of sacrifice by replacing them with the laws of love God and love thy neighbor.

The only passage in the New Testament regarding homosexuality that I am aware of states: ". . . the men . . . , having abandoned the natural use of the woman have burned in their lusts one towards another, men with men doing shameless things and receiving in themselves fitting recompense of their perversity" (Romans 1:27). Is this passage the inspired word of God? Or just a reflection of Leviticus from, or the personal opinion of, the author St. Paul? This statement I must consider seriously one way or the other. Yet, Christ said nothing in the Gospels regarding the subject of homosexuality. Furthermore, the inspired word of God is a topic beyond the scope of this book or my ability to comment.

It may seem easy enough for the heterosexual to address the homosexual with the task of refraining from his sexual leanings and live an otherwise normal life in all other aspects. After all many heterosexuals go through life without sexual activity, either by choice or by circumstances. But the heterosexual can always be buoyed by hope. If faced with immorality, the homosexual cannot hope for that dream of an intimate relationship and fulfillment of that intimacy. The dreaded fear of their justification may be at stake. If it is wrong, it is wrong. I will not contest the will of God. There may be some practical reason for homosexual activity being wrong, perhaps for our own benefit or safeguard. Aids comes to mind. At the time Scriptures were written knowledge of Aids was nonexistent.

There too is the Natural Law. Homosexuality may seem unnatural, or even disgusting, to many. It defeats God's primary purpose for sex, which is the creation and care of children: primary but not only. We cannot deny the mutual benefits of marriage to husband and wife who are unable, for one reason or another, to have children. Doesn't God bless those marriages equally with those who have children. Does the homosexual feel that their orientation is unnatural? Perhaps they feel their orientation is perfectly natural to them, only different. Let's face it: if they *were* born that way, isn't that by God's use of His powers of Nature to create them that way?

Platonic relationships between homosexuals should be acceptable, but, if true romantic feelings of love and sharing exist or develop, but must be denied, inevitable psychological hardship must follow. One can argue also that heterosexuals are not immune to similar psychological hardship of equal intensity as well.

What I wish to see is more data that lead to a fuller understanding of the case of homosexuality. Maybe then, and only then, can the subject be dealt with fairly and in line with the will of God. For now, I maintain that a complete understanding of God's law, the Natural Law, remains hidden from us. My intentions are not to defend homosexuality as moral, but to seek greater understanding of a very difficult situation that is a part of the lives of many of our citizens, an understanding that can hopefully lead to unity under God's will and away from the wide division that is growing in our society.

For the God-fearing homosexual, there must be a sense of urgency to clarify who they are and the direction they dare to take with sexual activity. Living what seems natural to them versus risking immorality in the face of the Almighty is an immense trauma. Understanding what this phenomena is cannot wait. They must know. We must join in the effort to understand this aspect of human diversity.

So, in summary: I don't know. I can only leave it at that. More insight would be helpful. United in our tolerance and respect for the homosexual is a good start, and acceptance of the truth God may reveal will take us down the right road toward understanding and toward what should be the response that God knows is best for all to follow.

Let us go into another issue here: one that has similarities, not necessarily with the same people, but similarities of how one may be led into a personal characteristic, one that can start innocently, such as a fulfillment of something gnawingly absent in one's life: the case of the pedophile. All it may take is a young child growing up discovering new psychological needs, like affection, love and being appreciated on a different level than at a younger age. The parents, who may have provided for those needs when a baby and beyond, may now find other pressing issues, important issues, like a job or new younger siblings. The affection and attention once monopolized are now redistributed.

All the child, or young adult, needs now is rejection. Some kids find new diversions, like sports, hobbies, school, scouting and the like, that absorb their focus and find appreciation or rejection for new talents discovered. Failure only adds to that gnawing lack of fulfillment. Another much younger and more innocent person seems to respond positively to those needs of the one deprived. And an innocent need for fulfillment today can grow into an increased focus of obsession, transforming an otherwise normal adult into something else. Then, what stands in the way of that obsession transforming a normal youth into a pedophile; or a homosexual, if in fact that can be applicable? Especially if no one can see it coming, not even that youth, except when he or she is suffering some form of emptiness or depression. It is a transformation that needs study, if it hasn't been done already. Then again, like the homosexual, there is the possibility that the condition is by birth. Residual harm done to others by the pedophile is far more serious than anything brought on by the homosexual.

Study of the adverse affects that come to the object of a pedophile's focus are well established and publicized today, but how much do we know about the pedophile himself, or even care. He has been demonized by the public, and rightly so for the harm his actions have done, but to the pedophile it has become another load of hot coals on the fire of rejection that all may have started quite innocently with the desperate need for filling a need.

So, as similar to the homosexual, more study is needed with regard to the pedophile. Little is known or understood for the same reasons. We are too often prone toward judging others whose problems we do not understand nor are faced to endure. Blame is easy, but solutions are not.

INFALLIBILITY

As a Catholic, I find the dogma of Infallibility to be a most difficult chapter to write, not that the subject has ever rested securely in the bosom of my heart. As a Catholic, however, I am required to believe that it is true. I, therefore, felt research on this most difficult subject would help me to clarify and understand it more fully.

To begin with I should indicate the importance it stands to play within the primary subject of this book: unity. I referred to the Catholic Resources website to begin my research and have found the following: "the Catholic Church, the Eastern and Oriental Orthodox churches, and the various Protestant denominations are divided by their views on Infallibility. The ecumenical movement, which hopes to reunify all of Christianity, has found that this is one of the most divisive of issues between churches." (page 5, http://en.wikipedia.org/wiki/Infallibility_of_the_Church)

Papal Infallibility does not define the pope as sinless, only without error in statements as defined below, as I interpret the issue to the best of my ability, which is not infallible.

Let's explore some statements taken from the Catholic Resources website:

"Papal Infallibility is a dogma of the Catholic Church which states that, by action of the Holy Spirit, the Pope is preserved from even the possibility of error when in his official capacity he solemnly declares or promulgates to the universal Church a dogmatic teaching on faith or morals." (page 1, http://en.wikipedia.org/wiki/Papal_infallibility)

Included in the dogma Munificentissimus Deus regarding the Assumption of Mary into heaven (see chapter on The Rosary): ". . . if anyone, which God forbid, should dare willfully to deny or call into doubt that which we have defined, let him know that he has fallen away completely from the divine and Catholic Faith." (page 11, http://www. ewtn.com/library/papaldoc/p12munif.htm) One might ask if infallibility applies to all 48 points of this dogma, including this one, or just those exactly applicable to Mary's Assumption into heaven.

Regarding Vatican II, "Pope John Paul II, summed it up when he completely contradicted the pre-conciliar Popes as follows.

"Freedom of conscience and of religion, including the aforementioned elements, is a primary and inalienable right of man." ("The Freedom of Conscience and of Religion", September 1, 1980)
http://www.romancatholicism.org/vatican-ii.htm

"Catholic theologians agree that the "1854 definition of the dogma of the Immaculate Conception of Mary and . . . 1450 definition of the dogma of the Assumption of Mary are instances of papal infallibility, . . . However, theologians disagree about what other documents qualify." (page 8, http://en.wikipedia.org/wiki/Papal_infallibility)

"The Holy See has given no list of papal statements considered to be infallible." (page 9, http://en.wikipedia.org/wiki/Papal_infallibility)

". . . before 1870 belief in papal infallibility was not a defined requirement of Catholic faith. The Church therefore accepted the oath required of Catholics in Ireland from 1793 for admittance of certain positions and which stated that 'it is not an article of Catholic Faith, neither am I thereby required to believe or profess that the Pope is infallible' The Irish bishops repeated their acceptance in a 25 January 1826 pastoral address to the Catholic clergy and laity in Ireland, stating: 'The Catholics of Ireland not only do not believe, but they declare upon oath . . . that it is not an article of the Catholic faith, nor are they required to believe, that the Pope is infallible, and that they do not hold themselves 'bound to obey any order in its own nature immoral', though the Pope or any ecclesiastical power should issue or direct such an order; but, on the contrary, that it would be sinful in them to pay any respect or obedience thereto.'" (page 10, http://en.wikipedia.org/wiki/Papal_infallibility) I am not of aware of any follow up on this declaration by any party to this date. Nor am I aware of any declaration of excommunication upon those Irish hierarchy for their statements afore mentioned.

For further confusion, I recommend review of all contents of the Catholic Resources websites on "papal infallibility" and "infallibility of the Church." I have taken the time to break down the complexities of the infallibility of the Church into an outline that follows the website description as best I can (see following page). I hope it may be helpful. For a more complete picture, review the website.

I am confident that the reader is finding the infallibility of the Catholic Church as clear and understandable as I do. To add to our bewilderment there have been many objections and denials as listed in the website, including:

"Pope John XXIII once remarked: 'I am only infallible if I speak infallibly, but I shall never do that, so I am not infallible.'"

Brian Tierney expressed the following: "'Pope John XXIII strongly resented the imputation of infallibility to his office—or at any rate to his predecessors. The theory of irreformability proposed by his adversaries was a 'pestiferous doctrine', he declared; and at first he seemed inclined to dismiss the whole idea as 'pernicious audacity'. However, through some uncharacteristic streak of caution or through sheer good luck (or bad luck) the actual terms he used in condemning the Franciscan position [on complete poverty of Christ and the Apostles] left a way open for later theologians to re-formulate the doctrine of infallibility in different language.'" (page 7, http://en.wikipedia.org/wiki/Papal_infallibility)

"Cardinal Newman . . . argues that conscience, which is supreme, is not in conflict with papal infallibility." (page 8, http://en.wikipedia.org/wiki/Papal_infallibility)

Christ said: "'. . . I say to thee, thou art Peter, and upon this rock I will build my church, and the gates of hell shall not prevail against it. And I will give thee the keys of the kingdom of heaven; and whatever thou shalt bind on earth shall be bound in heaven, and whatever thou shalt loose on earth shall be loosed in heaven.'" Matthew 16:18-19.

Robert E. Makara

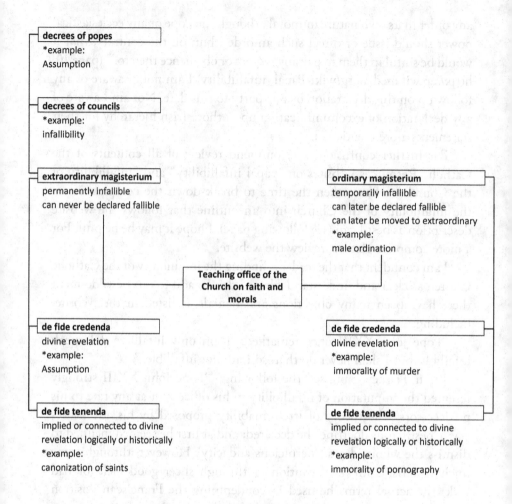

decrees of popes
*example:
Assumption

decrees of councils
*example:
infallibility

extraordinary magisterium
permanently infallible
can never be declared fallible

ordinary magisterium
temporarily infallible
can later be declared fallible
can later be moved to extraordinary
*example:
male ordination

Teaching office of the Church on faith and morals

de fide credenda
divine revelation
*example:
Assumption

de fide credenda
divine revelation
*example:
immorality of murder

de fide tenenda
implied or connected to divine
revelation logically or historically
*example:
canonization of saints

de fide tenenda
implied or connected to divine
revelation logically or historically
*example:
immorality of pornography

"James Robert White and others say that Matthew 16:18 does not refer to Peter as the Rock. They argue that in this passage Peter is in the second person ('you'), but that 'this rock', being in the third person refers to Christ, the subject of Peter's truth confession in verse 16, and the revelation referred to in verse 17, who is explicitly affirmed to be the foundation of the church. White cites Catholic authorities such as John Chrysostom and St. Augustine of Hippo as supporting this understanding, . . ." (page 12, http://en.wikipedia.org/wiki/Papal_infallibility) However, I might point out that the binding and the loosing is in the second person.

For additional objections and denials see the Catholic Resources website.

My research into the subject of infallibility has not come up with any satisfying answers. It appears that the 1870 definition of infallibility as being infallible has plunged the Church into a can of worms. Because of apparent confusion caused by complexity of the dogma, it would be beneficial to the membership of the Catholic Church, and other Christian believers and nonbelievers alike, to spell out with some understandable degree of simplicity what items infallibility entails, if that is possible. After all, this is what Catholics are required to believe. We Catholics are entitled to this. It is the responsibility of Catholic leadership to be "servant of all" (Mark 9:34), as pointed out by Jesus himself. And this is one important way it can and should carry out their duty. But it is understandable why a list has never been published: the complexities are too much for most of us to comprehend.

All efforts to seek any tolerance or compliance necessary among peoples of this world that may lead to unity were seriously jeopardized with the declaration of the infallibility of infallibility. Pope Boniface VIII's Bull Unam Sanctam of 1302 is considered "ex cathedra," infallible and irrevocably binding. This document "proclaimed that it is absolutely necessary for salvation that every human creature be subject to the Roman pontiff, pushing papal supremacy to its historical extreme." Extreme is right! To attribute this kind of statement, a determination on the behalf of God Almighty, as to who is saved and who is not, falls flat in the face of Jesus Christ's description of judgment, which deserves repeating here:

"'. . . and he will set the sheep on his right hand, but the goats on the left.

"'Then the king will say to those on his right hand, 'Come, blessed of my Father, take possession of the kingdom prepared for you from the foundation of the world; for I was hungry and you gave me to eat; I was thirsty and you gave me to drink; I was a stranger and you took me in; naked and you covered me; sick and you visited me; I was in prison and you came to me; . . . Amen I say to you, as long as you did it for one of these, the least of my brethren, you did it for me.' Then he will say to those on his left hand, 'Depart from me, accursed ones, into the everlasting fire which was prepared for the devil and his angels. For I was hungry, and you did not give me to eat; I was thirsty and you gave me no drink; I was a stranger and you did not take me in; naked and you did not clothe me; sick, and in prison, and you did not visit me.'" (Matthew 25:33-36, 40-43).

These charitable works are not exclusively attributable to "every human creature . . . subject to the Roman pontiff."

A close look at the kind of man Pope Boniface was is relevant. E. R. Chamberlain's book "The Bad Popes" describes extensively and in great detail what Boniface was all about. Chamberlain's book, on the other hand, contains so much elaborate detail that it raises the question of where he might derive all this without actually being there. I might question the validity of such knowledge. Nonetheless, the Catholic Resources website references his book, and more than once.

Pope Boniface VIII was, according to Chamberlain, desirous of the papacy, desirous of riches, pitted wealthy families against wealthy families for his own benefit, sent troops to destroy a city and kill thousands of inhabitants who disagreed with him, accused of simony and sodomy, loved pomp and power, involved himself in political affairs and intrigue usually for personal gain, sent adversaries into exile, and imprisoned his predecessor Pope Celestine V. But nobody is perfect. On his behalf, he did start a university, ordered unsuccessfully a truce between two Italian cities, had churches of Rome restored and spared the church, the only building remaining, in the city he destroyed. No doubt his reason for Unam Sanctam was to establish his own political power in Europe, without consideration for innocent and sincere people around the world. But who am I to judge, especially if he was guided by the Holy Spirit?

To find some justification for Unam Sanctam, we must research further, into the christianity-guide website. Here we find, in 1868, Pope Pius IX, two years prior to the declaration of the infallibility of infallibility, clarified the issue:

". . . this dogma (Unam Sanctam) has been misinterpreted by both Catholics and non-Catholics alike. Many popes stressed that those who are 'invincibly ignorant of the Catholic religion' can obtain salvation. Pope Pius IX stated in his encyclical Quanto conficiamur moeror (1868): 'We all know that those who are afflicted with invincible ignorance with regard to our holy religion, if they carefully keep the precepts of the natural law that have been written by God in the hearts of all men, if they are prepared to obey God, and if they lead a virtuous and dutiful life, can attain eternal life by the power of divine light and grace.'" (page 5, http://www.christianity-guide.com/christianity/pope.htm)

That's a relief. One must wonder about the traumatic concern sincere Catholics must have had for their non-Catholic brethren during the 566 year interim period between Unam Sanctam and the encyclical conficiamur moeror. Further reinforcement of the softening of Unam Sanctam came more recently:

"Pope John Paul II wrote in his encyclical Redemtoris Missio: 'But it is clear that today, as in the past, many people do not have the opportunity to come to know or accept the Gospel revelation or to enter the church. For such people, salvation in Christ is accessible by virtue of a grace which, by having a mysterious relationship to the church, does not make them formally a part of the Church but enlightens them in a way which is accommodated to their spiritual and material situation. This grace comes from Christ; it is the result of his sacrifice and is communicated by the Holy Spirit. It enables each person to attain salvation through his or her free cooperation.'" (page 5, http://www.christianity-guide.com/christianity/pope.htm)

These two encyclicals must bring comfort and understanding to Catholics and closer compliance with Matthew 25:33-36, 40-43. However, neither has ever been declared infallible. One may consider some possible clarification or denial of Cardinal Newman's statement regarding the supremacy of conscience. This view is capable of leading to all kinds of diverse interpretations, adding much to the dilemma of confusion.

"The Lord delivers the souls of his servants, nor will he be punished whoever flees to him for refuge." Psalms 33:23. "No one is condemned whose refuge is God." Psalms 34:23 (New American Bible).

At this point I may interject the following statement from Christ to the Pharisees: "'Have you not read what David did when he and those with him were hungry? how he entered the house of God, and ate the loaves of proposition which neither he nor those with him could lawfully eat, but only the priests? . . . I desire mercy, and not sacrifice, . . .'" (Matthew 12: 3-4,7).

Robert E. Makara

And when questioned about his curing on the Sabbath, Christ said: "'What man is there among you, if he has a single sheep and it falls into a pit on the Sabbath, will not take hold of it and lift it out.'" (Matthew 12: 11). Christ was interested in common sense and mercy, not laws that cannot be broken under any circumstances. The laws of love and mercy override laws of the Old Testament book of Leviticus. Read Leviticus, all of it; do we abide by these rules? All of them?

There is one option that the Catholic Church might take to alleviate significantly the confusion that infallibility has caused for believers who care enough or have the time to be concerned: Declare that the dogma of infallibility was a mistake. "For everyone who exalts himself shall be humbled, and he who humbles himself shall be exalted." Surely, it seems clear in which category the author of Unam Sanctam must set.

The beauty of this option is that in one clean stroke the pope can clear up all the confusion and conflict and avoid any wayward Church statements that may be promulgated in the future, or what has been promulgated in the past, statements that would require awkward interpretations and explanations to justify them. Other popes, of questionable moral character, seven in all, perhaps few in number for 2000 years of time, are discussed in Chamberlain's book.

On the down side, respect and prestige of the Catholic Church and effective leadership may suffer from world opinion for such an admission, but respect should grow in the eyes of most. The goal of unity among Christians would find significant inroads. Keep in mind, unity rests on mutual respect and the continuation of the search for truth by all, not conformity at any cost. Truth must stand as the eternal beacon we all seek.

Also, trust in the authority of the Church in other statements would suffer and may lead to total disregard by followers. Misinterpretations of Scripture would become commonplace without the guidance of the Holy Spirit through the Church. Doubt about the Catholic Church's leadership would rise up and never be lost. It's a tough situation. The fear of influences outside of Divine Inspiration will plague the Church with the question of how to decipher one from the other. Uneducated independent thinkers will go their own way. Much control over correct interpretation and leadership could become a thing of the past, resulting in chaos. Another pope like Boniface VIII is a fear as well, unlikely perhaps, but if it should ever happen, what kind of dogmas would he set forth? Fear stands to reign supreme.

70

By this chapter's discourse, I wish not to advocate the abandonment of infallibility, as too I do not advocate any recommendations for my own excommunication. I only want to point out some difficulties that exist for Christian believers, and thereby suggest that some help is needed in understanding the issue and what we are required to believe.

Below I have compiled a list of items suggested from a variety of fallible sources, for the sake of perspective and understanding, that have been declared infallible, incomplete and fallible that this list might be:

1. The Nicene Creed (all items contained therein)—Council of Nicaea—325 AD.
2. Mary is the mother of God—Council of Ephesus—431 AD.
3. Two natures of Christ—Council of Chalcaedon—451 AD.
4. Two wills of Christ—Third Council of Constantinople—680 AD.
5. No salvation unless subject to the Roman pontiff—Unam Sanctam—1302 AD.
6. Beatific Vision just prior to the Final Judgment—Benedictus Deus—1336 AD.
7. One God, three Persons—Contate Domino—1441 AD.
8. Perpetual virginity of Mary—Council of Trent—1564 AD.
9. Five propositions by Jansen condemned, including predestination—Cum Occasione—1563 AD.
10. Seven propositions of Jansen condemned, including every love that is not supernatural is evil—Unigenitus—1713 AD and Auctorem Fidei—1794 AD.
11. Immaculate Conception—Ineffabilis Deus—1854 AD.
12. Infallibility—Vatican Council—1870 AD.
13. Assumption—Munificentissimus Deus—1950 AD.

One might ask what is so important to the average Catholic that underlies the necessity of believing these items that have been declared infallible dogma. What is contained in the Creed is important to all of us and forms the foundation of our faith. The two natures and the two wills of Christ and three Persons in God are formulated out of Scripture by implication. Pope Boniface's Unam Sanctam has been significantly clarified (modified) by Pope Pius IX and Pope John Paul II. Anything that affects our final judgment is important; in fact, I can't think of anything more important. Predestination and human supernatural love only present serious consequences to all of us, if not condemned.

The virginity, Immaculate Conception and Assumption are important to Mary herself and traditional Catholics who consider them as most important in their devotions. They are without a doubt interesting and unique phenomena. What about average Catholics who are preoccupied with their daily lives and concerns and to progressive Catholics who worry more about the world's suffering and other earthly concerns? Whether or not these events ever happened may be the farthest from their minds. What may seem important to popes and bishops whose every day is involved with matters of faith may mean little to those involved with just doing what is right and meeting obligations of family, employment and attending Sunday Mass.

Belief in the Assumption was never a requirement until 1950. Before that, the burden of belief did not exist, if it is a burden. Now we have a new sin to avoid. I personally find the Assumption quite believable; it is not a burden. Anything is possible with God. But do I care? Maybe my lack of care is my sin. I begin to wonder if awareness of the mandate to believe this or that is beneficial. Or, is ignorance bliss? This brings us to the subject of our next chapter.

KNOWLEDGE

"The Lord God made to grow out of the ground all kinds of trees pleasant to the sight and good for food, the tree of life also in the midst of the garden, and the tree of the knowledge of good and evil." (Genesis 2:9). Ignorance was bliss.

Is it really true that ignorance is bliss? Did God tell Adam and Eve to *never* taste the fruit of the tree of knowledge? Evil misleads us away from its true essence, hiding the bad under the shade of the good, both in our day and in the past. The good may bask in the sun, but a *little* bit of knowledge hides the evil that lurks beneath for those who lack the full understanding of the consequences of our actions.

When we are children, we are disciplined to be good, but we are too young and naive to know the consequences until we are old enough to understand. Tell a child not to touch fire; he does not realize the bliss he enjoys until he disobeys and learns that excruciating pain lurks beneath the pretty glowing flames. He could have avoided this trauma if he had obeyed. When he is old enough, he will learn that the good is in being obedient. The story of Adam and Eve reveals this lesson, but I don't think God intends for us to be forever ignorant.

Adam and Eve would have never fallen to their temptation if they understood what they were getting themselves into, but it takes time to mature and learn. The consequences of failure to follow the easy path of obedience is likely to open the way for experience as a necessary option.

Ignorance is not bliss. All knowledge cannot be loaded onto our brains all at once. It takes time to grow. Knowledge will come in due time.

We are often tempted to disobey what we are taught. The Ten Commandments were brought to the Israelites by God through Moses. The Israelites suffered for their lack of obedience, as revealed in the Old Testament. We can learn by disobedience, by the difficult path. Those who transgress will hopefully learn from this path, and they in turn can become valuable teachers for those not yet old enough to understand.

Faith is important, but first truth, or something upon which to base faith, not blind faith. A terrorist has faith, but not based on the truth in spite of what he may think, based on a limited truth, beyond which the full truth is hidden from him. We cannot know the full truth, but enough to go on. Yet, one must always be ready and open to seek additional facts that may lead us to greater understanding. Partial truths can be misleading and dangerous.

I give credit to those who seek and use their minds, their consciences, the Natural Law to discover the truth, like Scott Hahn, who went through many trials in search of fulfillment in faith. They have used that wonderful gift that God gave to them, their minds, to search. Better off are they than those who may have been born into truth, never taking the time nor challenge to question, to search and to expand one's understanding, or even change one's thinking. Faith cannot be taken for granted. You never know: you may be stuck in fallacy, because of limited awareness.

We owe it to ourselves and others to seek understanding of other minds to share and strengthen their faith, and to draw others into the truth we may have to offer. To turn our backs on them is to turn our backs on Christ's command to teach all nations, and on ourselves by rejecting God's glorious gift of intellect by burying it in the ground out of fear, laziness or risk of contaminating our own faith systems. Therein lies the greater sin over innocent ignorance.

Christ maintained the essence of the Old Testament, but did change a great deal, including the laws of Leviticus and suggesting that we love our enemies. Such a liberal idea for his time! It is liberal still today.

We must be like children. We must admit humbly that we are limited and open our thoughts to follow what the Holy Spirit may be trying to tell us, usually through our consciences. The smartest people in the world are the ones most aware of how little they actually know. I believe, but I claim to know nothing. That makes me about as smart as anyone can get. Talk about arrogance!

"'Do not think that I have come to destroy the Law or the Prophets. I have not come to destroy, but to fulfill.'" Matthew 5:17. This brings us to the underlying subject of this chapter: Vatican II. Vatican II started with much enthusiasm and joy, but, it has become a catalyst for division between traditional and progressive Catholics. Progressives took the Council's lead and carried it onward to greater development, understanding and meaning for some, while traditionalists view the progressive movement as Vatican II Catholicism run amok. Whose right? This is where diversity and tolerance comes into play, on the part of both leaders and followers, but communication between the two sides must be maintained in order to uncover God's truth on critical matters of faith and morals and allow for the needs of all, without the attitude that "I am right," and no other way may be tolerated. Unnecessary intolerance is a sign of arrogance, and can only lead to resentment and division. At this point no one cares about any attempt at an understanding that may lead to tolerance and truth. Any hope for the kind of unity that Christ sought is lost.

The subject of conscience plays an important part here. "Pope Benedict XVI stated in 1982 that . . . . Those values, such as freedom of conscience, the liberty of other religions, a separation of Church from state and many other basic tenants of liberal pluralism had been repeatedly condemned by the Church, in particular by Pope Pius IX in his Syllabus of Modern Errors. Ratzinger wrote this:

' . . . we might say that (in conjunction with the texts on religious liberty and world religions) [Vatican II's Pastoral Constitution on the Church in the Modern World] is a revision of the Syllabus of Pius IX, a kind of countersyllabus . . . . Let us be content to say that the text serves as a countersyllabus and, as such, represents, on the part of the Church, an attempt at an official reconciliation with the new era inaugurated in 1789. [French Revolution] (Principles of Catholic Theology, 1987, pp. 381-2, Ignatius Press 1987)' (page 2, http://www.romancatholicism.org/vatican-ii.htm)

Those values are essential to the First Article of the United States Bill of Rights, I might add.

The Catholic Church, in many ways, could be accused of having become constricted by rules, and lost the way of Christ's simple commandments of

Love God and Love each other. He made clear to the Pharisees of his time that their strict religious regulations had become overbearing and fruitless.

The primacy of conscience makes sense. It only seems right that I believe that which my mind tells me is the truth. How can the conscience be denied? One thing that must always be kept in mind, however, is the realization that the conscience is based on a limited exposure to experiences in life, and, therefore, the conscience is easily prone towards false conclusions. The Holy Spirit does not mislead, but ignorance does. You may and should follow the beliefs of your conscience. But being a Christian or a Jew or a Moslem or an atheist or whatever does not mean closing your mind off to the thoughts and ideas of other people or any new evidence. That is not Christian or Jewish or Moslem or atheist or whatever, that's arrogant.

But he spoke this parable also to some who trusted in themselves as being just and despised others. "Two men went up to the temple to pray, the one a Pharisee and the other a publican. The Pharisee stood and began to pray thus within himself: 'O God, I thank thee that I am not like the rest of men, robbers, dishonest, adulterers, or even like this publican. I fast twice a week; I pay tithes of all that I possess.' But the publican, standing afar off, would not so much as lift up his eyes to heaven, but kept striking his breast, saying, 'O God, be merciful to me the sinner!'

"I tell you, this man went back to his home justified rather than the other; for everyone who exalts himself shall be humbled, and he who humbles himself shall be exalted." Luke 18:9-14.

Before becoming Pope Benedict XVI, Joseph Cardinal Ratzinger wrote:
. . . when the tax collector (publican) with all his undisputed sins is more righteous in the eyes of God than the Pharisee with all his genuinely good deeds (Luke 18:9-14), this is not because the sins of the tax collector were not sins or the good deeds of the Pharisee not good deeds . . . . The Pharisee is no longer aware that he too is guilty. He is perfectly at ease with his own conscience. But this silence of his conscience makes it impossible for God and men to penetrate his carapace [the bony shield that covers the back

of some animals]—whereas the cry of conscience that torments the tax collector opens him to receive truth and love. Jesus can work effectively among sinners because they have not become inaccessible behind the screen of an erring conscience, . . . their conscience no longer accuses them but only justifies them. (p. 81-82, "Values in a Time of Upheaval" by Joseph Cardinal Ratzinger)

Why is it much easier to love the vulnerable than it is to love the powerful? We may admire or respect the strong, but we love the weak as long as we can understand their cause. It is difficult to understand the strong probably because we are not able to understand how they are what they are. No one, however, is perfect. If we truly understood the powerful, we may see their weaknesses and thereby love them as well. We will love what we can relate to, what we may recognize in ourselves, our own weaknesses. God created each one of us with individual weaknesses. When we turn a blind eye to them and take pride in our strengths, we cannot share in the joy of God's love for us. In stead, we love ourselves, not God. God loves us all because he is all knowing, and therefore understands us all perfectly. If we can accept our own weaknesses, we can accept the love of God. Our strengths are a matter of thanksgiving on our part, not pride. In fact, our weaknesses can be a matter of thanksgiving on our part, not shame.

Joseph Cardinal Ratzinger continued:

To put this in other terms, the identification of conscience with the superficial conscience and the reduction of man to his subjectivity do not liberate but rather enslave. They do this by making us completely dependent on prevailing opinions, indeed lowering the level of these opinions day by day . . . the reduction of conscience to a subjective certainty means the removal of truth. (p. 83, "Values in a Time of Upheaval" by Joseph Cardinal Ratzinger)

The theory of relativism implies righteousness is flexible and variable from one person to the next. This theory leads us to qualify what is right from conclusions taken from one's limited exposure. Limited exposure can be misleading. If I am exposed to one percent of all life's possibilities, an extraordinary high percentage for just one person, then the 99 percent remaining may lead toward the opposite line of thinking and therefore my beliefs are subject to questioning. But the other 99 percent must then be discarded, because they are not in line with my conscience. You see the danger here? If my conscience says it's ok for me to cheat, harm or offend my neighbor in some way, I may feel justified, but my neighbor is still cheated, or harmed, or offended. Is that ok?

Conscience may merit primacy, but that conscience must be prepared to seek further exposure to a greater understanding when doubt appears. Certainty can never in a life time reach 100 percent. When I die, and find myself in God's presence, he may enlighten me to 100 percent certainty, then and only then. Otherwise, I can know nothing with 100 percent certainty. People who say they do scare me. The person who thinks he knows everything can never learn anything. It is possible that some people have been enlightened by the Holy Spirit, maybe the pope, but I don't know that 100 percent. We can only trust and hope we are following the will of God.

It is easy to be mislead over the impact of eternal life and the threat of its fears when people insist you must do this or do that or lose your immortal soul to damnation or away from its promises. It is fear that drives the potential terrorist into action; a fear based on exposure that is highly limited and seriously flawed. The leaders of young unsuspecting candidates for terrorism may be led in turn by the same fears, all initiated by someone to carry out relief of his own false interpretation of an idea or satisfaction of passions of hate or outrage or other reaction that represents perceived justice for limited, but very real experiences.

One major benefit to opening up a subject of controversy to dialogue is the possibility of one side changing opinion from wrong to right, hopefully not right to wrong, or at least increasing understanding of opposing opinions. Broadening one's scope of insight is always beneficial and can only lead to a greater chance of peace and love for one another.

This does not mean it is easy to change and admit to having been wrong or shallow in one's understanding. Change is very difficult. It may take a lifetime, but it is a part of growth in knowledge, understanding and personal maturity. Change takes humility and courage. One cannot, and should not, deny past influences. There still remains a possibility of waffling opinion back and forth. Controversial subjects are complex. We must always remain open to new evidence. One thing we must remain clear of is the temptation to become biased toward all facets of an opinion simply because one facet appears to be wrong.

In summary, a little bit of knowledge can be a very dangerous thing. More is better, but always beware. In the case of the terrorist who is convinced that what he is about to do is a good thing, he might find 70 young virgins an enticing drawing card for any action if he really believes it and is convinced that it is 100 percent true, in his mind of narrow awareness. But 70 young virgins may become severely tiresome after the first one billion millenniums of eternity, if not long before. Such is the fallacy of short term goals.

The Catholic Church could be held responsible for following in the footsteps of the Pharisees of Jesus' time by getting bogged down over rules and regulations, that Vatican II tried to loosen up. We depend on the Church for guidance. Surely, we are in need of it for clarity of mind and elimination of unnecessary confusion, especially where modern day issues that never existed in years past have risen to confront us in our current way of life; issues that keep appearing at an accelerated pace like never before. But rigid regulations that harness believers to proper procedures and habitual exercises and rituals under pain of sin, or even mortal sin, do not follow in the teachings of Jesus Christ. Regulations may be good in themselves, but more reflective of burdens to be carried borne out of fear of punishment than for love of our God.

However, for too many of us, if dutiful requirements are not demanded, nothing in the way of sacrifice, devotion, Mass attendance, etc. would ever be done at all. It is too easy to ignore an oftentimes apparent invisible God, and attend to our daily lives and more tempting pleasurable pastimes. Mass attendance and other communal prayer opportunities are being ignored by members of the faith whether they are binding or not. Voluntary acts are done out of love. The intentions of many to carry out binding acts are rooted in fear of consequences.

Non-Catholic Christians do not bind their congregations to attend Sunday services. We know that their hearts are in the right place. The problem is too many just don't care these days and don't practice any religious form of life. They may be honest perhaps, but to close themselves off from any prayerful life or relationship to a higher Being is to close themselves off from needed psychological advantages that will arise someday. How does one pray when a habit of faith is lacking compared with believers who have practiced their faith through crises of the past? Crises lurk in our future that may never cause any concern today.

A good example of Catholic regulations is abstaining from eating meat on Fridays. This may be a good practice as a devotion to God, but under the pain of mortal sin that condemns the abuser to eternal damnation without remorse or a good confession? Shouldn't we leave heaven and hell up to God? Christ did give Peter, as head of the Church, the power to loose and to bind, so who am I to say? Abstaining from meat was never any sacrifice for me. I have always liked fish better than meat anyway. I used to look forward to Fridays. This regulation served no devotional purpose for me; so much for rules and regulations. Guidelines, yes, but practicing devotion to God may vary from one person to the next.

The Pharisees " . . . asked him, saying, 'Is it lawful to cure on the Sabbath?' that they might accuse him. But he said to them, 'What man is there among you who, if he has a single sheep and it falls into a pit on the Sabbath, will not take hold of it and lift it out? . . . Therefore, it is lawful to do good on the Sabbath.'" Matthew 12:10-12.

Jesus said: "'I desire mercy, and not sacrifice.'" Matthew 9:13.

Jesus proclaimed two overriding commandments and they cover everything, including the original ten God passed on through Moses. He called for little in the way of rigid details. It is better that we show our love of God and neighbor voluntarily. Finding that love for God is all too often forgotten, the Church set up the arbitrary requirement for all Catholics to abstain from meat on Fridays. At least that's the way it used to be. Vatican II dropped this regulation under the condition that doing something charitable be done in its place. A requirement still continues, but most Catholics are unaware of the added condition that excuses not eating meat. The Eastern Rite of the Catholic Church still continues the abstinence from meat on Fridays regulation. Voluntary acts are signs of true love.

Vatican II participants felt that we should not be bound by rules, but should show a more mature Christian devotion to God by doing sacrifice or charitable acts on our own, voluntarily. This would be better, so they thought, but they overestimated the spiritual maturity of their membership. Even the most sincere of Catholics prefer to be told what to do. People do not want to think for themselves. It is easier to follow the book. Unfortunately, following the book has worked little maturity into our spirituality over all these years, and centuries.

Jesus brought us the two great commandments, a perfectly simple and all encompassing pair of requirements for living, that can be applied to every new situation that may face us throughout the centuries; past, present and future. It's up to us to allow the Holy Spirit to guide us in developing the details based on love.

Even Albert Einstein could not bring himself to discover a simple universal equation that could govern all aspects of the physical world. Isaac Newton discovered simple laws of gravity that served man scientifically for centuries until Einstein unveiled new knowledge that proved that Newton was not completely right. Newton did not know about Einstein's Theory of Relatively. Einstein never achieved his goal of finding this universal equation that would combine gravity and electromagnetism into one equation. He didn't know about Quantum Mechanics. His Theory of Relativity was not completely right either. Now they believe that a new theory of vibrating strings are what unifies gravity, electromagnetism and the forces that hold the atomic nucleus together. What next?

But, before we go any further and reveal my ignorance of modern physics, the point I am trying to make here is that knowledge is to be revealed in due time, on schedule, as God only knows. Isaac Newton found a smooth stone on the beach; Einstein captured a cup of the ocean; the beach and the ocean of God's truth remains to be revealed to us through eternity. My God, I love you!

Vatican II was not infallible, nor did it declare any part of the discussions and declarations as such, but ". . . Pope Paul VI stated: *'all that has been established synodally is to be religiously observed'*, he was making all the Council texts a matter of *'religious submission'* which is what is given to non-infallible matter." (page 4, http://www.romancatholicism. org/vatican-ii.htm) Observed under pain of what, I do not know. The Catholic Church has suffered from division ever since: the progressives loved the opening up to a new vision, while traditionalists decried excesses and confusion.

Pope Paul VI stated: "We looked forward to a flowering, a serene expansion of conceptions which matured in the great sessions of the Council. But one must notice above all the sorrowful aspect. It is as if the Church were destroying herself." (Address to the Lombard Seminary at Rome, December 7, 1968)

And "Indeed, the extent and depth of the teaching of the Second Vatican council call for a renewed commitment to deeper study in order to reveal clearly the Council's continuity with Tradition, especially in points of doctrine which, perhaps because they are new, have not yet been well understood by some sections of the Church," (Ecclesia Dei, 1988). To add to the confusion, "Pius IX defined that a Pope cannot make new doctrine but John Paul II claimed that the Popes of Vatican II did just that." (page 6, http://www.romancatholicism.org/vatican-ii.htm)

Walter M. Abbott, SJ, adds:

> "And last of all it was the most opportune, because, bearing in mind the necessities of the present day, <u>above all it sought to meet the pastoral needs</u> and, nourishing the flame of charity, it has made a great effort to reach not only the Christians still separated from communion with the Holy See, but also the whole human family." (*In Spiritu Sancto*, Walter M. Abbott, SJ, The Documents of Vatican II, pp. 738-9).

The Church wanted to open dialogue with non-Catholics and the world at large, and keep the Council's conclusions open for future study. Vatican II was not final, but a beginning. Stay tuned for Vatican III? The sequel? The next cup to be revealed from the ocean of God's spiritual truth? Confusion and hope. I see it as a part of growing pains; growing into another era. Vatican II has opened the can of worms and it has begun to fester, but the Holy Spirit will direct us into a bright future of eventual growth and maturity for all of us after the pain of sorting it all out has subsided. Let us hope that the Catholic hierarchy on both sides will adopt the tolerance necessary to bring all believers, including themselves, together for the firm purpose of discovering God's truth and, eventually, understanding and unity.

Like the fruit of the knowledge of good and evil, Vatican II revealed a truth: the broad disunity among Catholics about where the Church is and should be. We all must receive knowledge in due time. Unfortunately, that time varies from one person to the next. For some, Vatican II was too early. For others, it was too late. When Vatican III comes to another level, hopefully it can bring God's truth securely to all of us, and its clarity will bring us all together, both traditionalists and progressives, in the unity of God's truth. I hope it's not too late . . . or too soon.

EAST AND WEST

Originally, this chapter was to be called East vs. West because of elements of conflict that have presented themselves, but, to be more positive, I have replaced "vs." with "and." My view of the two divisions of the Catholic Church may be a narrow one.

There are two primary divisions within the Catholic Church, both under the jurisdiction of the Pope in Rome: the Eastern Rite and the Roman Rite. From my experience with members and practices of each, I have generated some (fallible) opinions regarding the two, how they differ, and how they regard each other. I am sure others may have a more thorough and accurate perspective to offer. But, nevertheless, here goes.

The most obvious difference is the East is more conservative and the Roman more liberal. Results of Vatican II are more favorable in the Roman Rite. Some members of the Eastern Rite are critical of Roman practices and procedures. Where the Roman Rite predominates, such as in the United States, Roman Catholics tend to ignore the Eastern churches. Most Roman Catholics here know little about the less common Eastern churches.

Another difference, a shade of a difference, is the emphasis on the two great commandments of love. Both rites consider both 1) love of God and 2) love of each other as essential, but the Eastern Rite focuses a little more on worshiping God while the Roman Rite focuses a little more on how we treat one another. This is just my own personal, although narrow, perspective.

The Eastern Rite puts greater importance on the procedures and details of the liturgy, while the Roman Rite gives greater flexibility in allowing variations in how the liturgy is conducted. The faith of the more conservative Roman Catholic would resemble that of the Eastern Catholic in this regard.

One may argue whether this is true or not but it is my feeling that the division in Christian churches is a matter of fear versus pride, the underlying problems that generate conservative versus liberal.

In the Catholic religion conservatives have resented and resisted the imposition of change, such as what followed from Vatican II. Change from what they grew up with, grew comfortable with and accepted with their whole hearts seems to fly in the face of their true faith. Liberals, who have grasped change, saw it as more meaningful to them and now resent or ignore any efforts by conservatives who are trying to reverse changes back to the way it was, which flies in the face of their aspirations for a growing evolving church. Conservatives are too afraid to move forward and liberals are too proud to step backward. I am not talking about morals and the teachings of God that cannot be reversed. It's the details, in how we worship, for example. Does it matter how we receive Communion, by hand or by mouth? Is there something wrong with the Tridentine Mass? What's wrong with the guitar and other instruments during liturgy? Let us be tolerant of one another. For most, I believe we are. For some, whether it be based on fear or pride, we need a little more love and tolerance.

A favorite of the traditional Roman Catholic is the love for the Latin Tridentine Liturgy. At one time Mass was never spoken in English, only in the Latin language, which no one anywhere ever speaks in daily conversation. It is a dead language. But it was the excepted tongue of the liturgy of the Mass as I was growing up in the 1950's. The correct meaning of the words could not be accurately translated into English I was told. So, it was better that the congregation understand none of the words rather than inaccurately. Most missals contained the liturgical prayers in Latin on the left side and the English translation on the right, thereby one could follow along and understand the only meaning the person is capable of understanding by looking back and forth, an understanding that was inaccurate nonetheless.

Trying to explain the Latin meaning to an English-speaking person is futile if it cannot be done. Consequently, English-speaking people must go through life in ignorance of the true liturgical meaning; otherwise, any translated explanation should be able to be used as the basis for an accurate translation of liturgical prayers. Why not? I simply do not nor ever did understand what I was told back in the 1950's.

The apparent reason why traditional Catholics are attracted to the Latin Mass is the nostalgia of what they grew up with. It gives a more comforting and religious feeling to their worship. It just seems more sacred. Which is ok. Church worship should provide a religious experience. I'm not sure how to define a religious experience. It surely varies from person to person. It must be the inspiration that leads us to follow in the spiritual life that Christ established for us.

Liturgies in other languages have always maintained an experience that worshipers seek, without resorting to a dead language. In the Ukraine, for instance, the native language is used, not Latin. The Latin Mass in the United States has become more common recently. At one time, since Vatican II, the Latin Mass could be conducted by permission only. Why?

It was by luck that I arrived one day in 2006 at Guadalupe, the famous shrine in Mexico City, just in time for the celebration of Mass in the Aztec language. It had been recently approved by Pope John Paul II. The local instruments, the colorful vestments, the lyrical rhythms, the subdued dance at the exit of the priest and other participants, all contributed to a beautiful event. I loved it. It was more elaborate than usual, because of the location of this special event, but within regulations that define it as a celebration of the Catholic Mass. The lover of the Latin Mass might have found it a shock.

Likewise, if the progressive Catholic prefers something they feel is more meaningful to them, then so be it, as long as it gives the inspiration that leads one to follow in the spiritual life that Christ established and stays within limitations beyond which such freedom becomes license and loses resemblance to the reenactment of the Last Supper, the unbloody sacrifice of Christ's Body and Blood. Some guidelines are necessary. It is not for me to dictate what they should be. Unfortunately, therein lies the grounds where conflict between traditional and progressive begin. It is often a matter of "taste," as one Franciscan told me.

The traditional and progressive would do well to accept, or at least tolerate, the tastes of each other's liturgies, even embrace them. What is disrespectful to one may be inspirational to the other. What is boring and tiresome to the other may be sacred to the one. A negative and critical attitude is not helpful and borders on arrogance. If there exist irreconcilable differences, let's agree to disagree, and get on with life. How we worship should not condemn the importance that we all do worship in good faith the best way we know how.

THE ROSARY

The rosary is regarded by traditional Catholics as sacred, putting it right up there at the top of the list of divinely inspired forms of prayer. The Our Father is included six times during the course of one five-decade rosary. The Our Father was given to us by Jesus during his Sermon on the Mount. The Hail Mary is repeated 53 times during the same five-decade sequence. The first sentence of the Hail Mary was given to us by the angel Gabriel and the second sentence by Mary's cousin Elizabeth when Mary visited her during Elizabeth's sixth month of pregnancy with John the Baptist. The third sentence was added later, probably by St. Benedict.

The combination of these prayers to form what is called the rosary was given to us also by St. Benedict. Its recital, daily for world peace and conversion of Russia, has been strongly encouraged by Mary during many of her recent appearances. The Catholic Church regards many of these appearances as real, but not all. In any case, the Church does not require its membership to accept any of them as infallible and therefore required by faith. The progressive Catholic may regard these appearances as interesting, but of little importance in the formation and inspiration of their spiritual life. Traditional Catholics consider them much more important, and will vouch for the power of praying the rosary. Daily recital is required by many orders of priests and nuns.

The rosary's individual prayers are great, but the problem, as I see it, is repetition. Saying the same words over and over, day after day, is monotonous. Better to use meditation and let the mind flow with the inspiration of the Holy Spirit. Why keep repeating these same words? It seems too much like a formula, like this particular combination is more pleasing to God than any other. Even Jesus said in Matthew 6:7-8: "But in praying, do not multiply words, as the Gentiles do; for they think by saying a great deal, they will be heard. So don't be like them; for your Father knows what you need before you ask him." Nevertheless, he may have intended this statement for prayers of petition (he "knows what you need"), as opposed to other forms, such as thanksgiving, adoration and penance. Also, Christ may have meant that we are not to pray mindlessly by repetition without thinking about what we are saying.

One other difficulty with the rosary is what do we focus upon in prayer? Should I think about the intentions for which I pray, or do I focus upon the words of these repeated prayers, or, what I find more satisfying, meditating upon the so-called mysteries, allotted to each decade. There are four separate sets of five, generally allotted to particular days of the week: the five Joyful to Monday and Saturday, the five Luminous to Thursday, the five Sorrowful to Tuesday and Friday, and the five Glorious to Sunday and Wednesday. Or focus upon what ever stirs the mind and heart. I can only think about one thing at a time. I suspect most people are the same.

Some will say the rosary while doing mundane chores or driving the car. I don't see much benefit from saying it while doing a crossword puzzle, my income tax or anything that totally distracts my attention. Better, of course, to clear the mind and pray, whatever form of prayer one chooses, without any distraction. Some, especially in years past, have pulled out their beads during Mass liturgy. There is definitely a distraction here, away from the Mass celebration. Perhaps I shouldn't criticize. Maybe some people *can* focus fully on two separate thoughts, but I can't.

Whatever focus and circumstances by which one prays, the rosary *does* form a discipline of taking the time to spend in prayer. Jesus told the disciples that they "must always pray and do not lose heart." Luke 18:1. The habit of devoting time each day to prayer and recognition of God is important.

During the times I have recited the rosary, I have focused upon the mysteries and it has led me to form numerous thoughts, questions, answers, insights and even doubts on these events. Let us spend some time in more detail regarding the Mysteries of the Rosary. Most of the events they contain are held dear to members of all Christian faiths. They are treated in chronological order.

Joyful Mysteries:

1. The Annunciation.

The angel Gabriel announces to Mary that she will give birth to the Savior promised by prophets years before. ". . . the Lord hath comforted his people, he hath redeemed Jerusalem. The Lord hath prepared his holy arm in the sight of all the Gentiles, and all the ends of the earth shall see the salvation of our God." Isaiah 52: 9-10.

Angelic appearances to humans are mentioned elsewhere in Scripture, both the Old Testament and the New, such as the appearance to the shepherds on the night of Jesus' birth and the three appearances to St. Joseph. One might ask why we never hear about angelic appearances today. Good question.

The Catholic Church has noted appearances by Mary, but not all are accepted. Traditional Catholics take them seriously, pointing to miraculous cures, for instance, at appearance sites, as the many crutches hanging in the shrine churches should attest. Progressives adjust their focus elsewhere, seemingly more real, like peace and justice through the political system. A progressive may think twice about miracles when faced with terminal illness. Traditionals say "pray for peace," while progressives say "work for peace," but their prayers for peace may be answered when God provides more workers for peace. Human history indicates a lack of prayer, or a lack of workers, or, more likely, a lack of both, as no lack of war over the centuries should attest. Once again, mutual support makes sense. Prayer and work should become a unified effort.

I have never witnessed a miraculous appearance, but that doesn't eliminate the possibility. But let's face it: they are rare.

It would be of intense worldwide interest if Mary had written a book about her experiences. Think about it, a written record about all her feelings and reactions throughout an intimate life with her son Jesus. There is little known about Jesus until he began his ministry. It could have been an all-time best-seller, second only to the Bible.

What did she see when the angel appeared to her? Did the angel look human? Did he have wings? Where did the idea of angels having wings come from? Famous paintings from centuries ago showed them with wings. The Old Testament describes carvings on the Ark of the Covenant portraying angels with wings. What do angels need wings for? Do they fly? Or are they spiritual? It would have been great to hear Mary's story. She surely saw something. How did she feel? A well-known Hollywood movie portrayed Mary's reactions by focusing on her and not showing the angel Gabriel at all, hiding the fact that the filmmakers didn't know either.

Mary must have communicated to Matthew and Luke what had happened, perhaps through others. Also, how did she know that the angel's name was Gabriel? He must have told her so. No name was given to the angels who made appearances in the Old Testament.

Detailed introspective discussion may seem irrelevant to our central theme of unity, but it can be a source of reflection even for the most progressive Catholic, or a source of criticism by unbelievers who seek arguments through questions we cannot answer. And a fuller understanding of what the rosary can be may lead closer toward unity and unbelievers toward appreciation.

The Annunciation demonstrates Mary's constant preparation to orient her life to God, to do His will over her own plans. This should be our attitude as well, but we all know how difficult it is to redirect ourselves when plans and dreams of our own are blocked. Our focus should be God. It may not fit our best interests for now but, in the long run, as we do our best to do God's will, it all works out to our best interests eventually.

It will at times be difficult to determine what exactly God is trying to say to us about what His will for us is. Research, consultation, meditation, prayer and an attitude of humility and sacrifice are all valuable factors that enable us to discover the right path.

2. The Visitation.

What makes the Visitation significant to us? It is of great importance to realize the plight of many people in this world who are lonely, abandoned, needy, sick, etc. For many of us who are busy in our productive years, we find little time for others. It may even be our mothers and fathers. Put them away in nursing homes and forget about them. Although not all of us offspring are so negligent, many, unfortunately for the tossed-aside parents, are too absorbed in other things or live too far away. Then, someday we too reach that tossed-aside age. The pattern of how we treated our parents has been established in the lifestyles of our own offspring, and . . . guess what. It all comes down to charity. It can be family, the lady next door or some starving person thousands of miles away, but it all comes down to charity, and making ourselves aware is an important stepping stone towards being charitable.

Mary's visit to her cousin was a charitable act, a time to be helpful to a family member, just to be there, and to share. And it was no small journey to visit Elizabeth. It is at least 40 miles (63 km) to the nearest edge of Judah, plus the additional distance to that particular town in Judah, which is not specifically mentioned. There was no transit system in those days. She probably walked or rode on the back of an animal, requiring a significant effort by our standards.

Mary pays a three month visit to her cousin Elizabeth in a town of Judah. A skeptic may point to her disappearance from her hometown as an attempt to hide a pregnancy out of wedlock, but her visit took place during her first three months. She was home for the last six. This doesn't overlook the likely humiliation she must have suffered at the hands of hometown villagers. It was a no-win situation. How much of a quizzical eye did she receive? Who would believe her? "I am a virgin made pregnant by the Holy Spirit of God." We have no account of this period in her life, but a little imagination points up to another way Mary must have suffered.

Where was Joseph in all this? We know that he was betrothed to Mary when she was in late pregnancy, but stayed with her after the angel reassured him of what happened. He too must have suffered some ridicule as well, but his faith carried him through and preserved their future marriage. One wonders why Mary did not tell Joseph about the angel's visit to her prior to this. Maybe she did, but he may have brushed it off as some fantasy or a joke. Who knows?

What makes the Visitation significant as a Mystery is the leap of joy that came from John the Baptist in Elizabeth's womb upon Mary's arrival. Also significant is Elizabeth's coining of the first half of the Hail Mary prayer. Evidence of the use of these words in prayer has survived as graffiti at Christian sites as early as the Second Century.

3. The Birth of Our Lord.

There isn't anything really mysterious about giving birth anymore than the miracle of birth that resounds throughout history, but this birth is exceptional beyond imagination: Christ, God, has incarnated as a physical human creation, a man, but also God. What can be more extraordinary? And he did it out of a complete giving . . . to us. Think about that when giving at Christmas.

One question that intrigues me is how aware was the Christ child at birth? Did he know that he was God? It seems hard to believe that God didn't know that he was God. Or did he grow into the awareness of who he was like any other child? What happened, happened. Perhaps it is not important one way or the other, but it is an interesting question to say the least.

Did he know that he was going to suffer? Or did his human nature dominate at this tender age while his knowledge and awareness of who he was and where he was headed grew as he matured as a human being. As an adult he was able to see the future, that he must suffer, that Peter would deny Christ three times and would have to go where he did not want to go, etc. We will return to this question for the Sorrowful Mysteries.

There is much to be said about this unique birth, not much that hasn't been said before, and forgotten by most when the Christmas season rolls around. But my imagination, bringing up that familiar scene in the stable over two thousand years ago, visualizes something more now in powerful symbolism than I was ever aware of before, perhaps because of my own ignorance and blindness over all these years.

Yes, Christ was born in poverty. And whether the three kings from the east visited the Holy Family that night or years later, as some historians suggest, this traditional setting has survived from the year 1223 when St. Francis of Assisi began popularizing it. We see the crib scene somewhere every Christmas, but it says much more than a reminder of how the holiday tradition began. The presence of wealth tells us that wealth in itself is not condemned. It depends on what we do with it, like sharing it as gifts of charity with those in need, and leaving it all behind to travel on a long journey in search of what is really important, in this case, the simplicity and promise of a little child and the hope of a better future that one day that child would bring. Even the evil intention of King Herod could not circumvent the three kings from their mission, thanks to the miracles of a dream and the angel's intervention. (See Matthew 2: 7-18.)

And poverty is present, not just in the circumstances surrounding this setting, but in the lowly shepherds who are invited by an angel to share in the wonder of this momentous night. The presence of both rich and poor is symbolic of togetherness . . . unity. Is the mix of these extremes a sign that we are all together here in a world where what we own is not where it's at? Provision of basic needs we are all entitled to can be achieved by working together, not by separation of rich and poor, where compassion seems no longer necessary because: what I don't know won't hurt me. Do we need an angel's invitation?

And the animals. There were probably more animals present at Christ's birth than humans. It is incredible the contribution animals make in service of our needs. It is shocking how much of this we take for granted, and what little appreciation most of them get in return.

Who could have orchestrated this beautiful setting? The creativity. The originality. The power. The irony.

. . . God?

4. The Presentation of Our Lord in the Temple.

Presentation of a young child is an introductory religious ceremony and Jewish custom that is still practiced today by Orthodox and Conservative Jews at about 40 days after birth, and is now called Pidyon Haben. It follows the rules of Leviticus in memory of the redemption of the first-born male from slaughter during the time of Moses and Egyptian slavery, and a carrying out of a purification of the mother and her blood following birth. This indicates that Mary and Joseph were dutifully practicing their Judaic religion.

One may question why this event should be identified as a mystery. The mystery surrounding the Presentation involves secondary occurrences accompanying Christ's Presentation, by two other people, that is extraordinary.

One, an old holy man named Simeon said that the Holy Spirit had informed him that he would not die until he saw the Savior. The promise was then fulfilled. The other, a holy woman and prophetess named Anna, who was constantly in the Temple, came to give praise. She had been speaking to many people of Jesus' coming. These two must have given Mary and Joseph much confidence and reassurance of who Jesus was and the important roll Mary was to play. Simeon, however, also informs Mary that "thy soul a sword shall pierce." This discomforting bit of news was revealed, I would think, to prepare Mary for the horrible death that her son must endure in her presence. Joseph was not included, seemingly indicating that he would not be there. As for what happened to him, there again is no indication.

5. The Finding of Our Lord in the Temple.

This is one mystery I do not like, and never have. That may be because of the way it is described in chapter 2 of Luke's Gospel, or the way it has been translated. Not knowing the full picture, it is difficult to make judgment.

It is difficult to understand how Mary and Joseph could possibly have left Jerusalem without their son at their side, or even knowing exactly where he was for a whole day before discovering he was not with them.

The sketchy information Luke gives indicates to me some degree of negligence on the part of Mary and Joseph. Was Jesus that independent at age twelve? Surely, if Jesus was truly divine and was aware of this at that young age, shouldn't he have been aware of his parents' departure? Then to respond to Mary the way he did when she asked why he stayed at the Temple to speak with religious leaders while they were going home: "Did you not know that I must be about my Father's business?" On the surface, it indicates an obstinate little boy. I would not make this kind of judgment of Christ, even at that age, so I must assume the lack of a clear picture of what happened. It seems that staying in the Temple was more important than the distress he was putting his parents through.

One thing is clear: Mary and Joseph were filled with joy when they found him. Any self-respecting mother of today would have given the child a good scolding, except for the joy of finding him that would outweigh any need for disciplinary action. Another aspect is the indication of Mary's profound sense of humility. She must have had a sense of perspective as to who Jesus was in order to keep "all these things carefully in her heart." Luke 2:51

Like most moments of joy in our lives, there is, has been or is about to be some form of pain that spikes the joy that we feel. It is, for some reason or another, the very nature of life. In the Visitation Mary's wonder and joy is accompanied by apprehension and uncertainty. The joy of the visit with her beloved cousin Elizabeth is burdened by her upcoming return to Nazareth, pregnant and open to neighbors' gossip. And the joy of Jesus' birth is preceded by her first experience of the traditional pains of giving birth. The joy of the Presentation is spiked by Simon's message: "Thy soul a sword shall pierce." Finally, the joy of finding Jesus is preceded by the horror of his absence, the return journey to Jerusalem and panic in search of her son.

The foregoing discussion is a result of focus and meditation, much of it while saying the Rosary. Questions that come to mind may raise some doubt of the reality of these mysteries. I share these thoughts in hope of stirring up some answers from the readers. They beg for answers, but not that doubt over minor matters should reduce anyone's faith. We don't know everything. A lack of information and full understanding in no way should affect foundation of faith. The message of love Jesus Christ gave us is far more important than the relative insignificance of these items.

Luminous Mysteries:

We move on to the Luminous Mysteries. If you prayed the Rosary 20 years ago, you never recited it with this set of mysteries in mind, because Pope John Paul II had not yet initiated them as the fourth set. They maintain the chronological order already established by the other three. The Luminous Mysteries fit in neatly between the Joyful and the Sorrowful, during Christ's ministry years prior to his Passion and Death, from ages 29 through 32. For the period between ages 12 through 29, very little, unfortunately, is known. Mary's book, if she wrote one, or one by Joseph, may have been the only possible sources for a fifth set.

1. The Baptism of Jesus.

Symbolism, such as what represents our baptism, may seem to have little affect on our daily lives and concerns. Symbolism lacks concrete relevance, but when you consider what it may be like without events like baptism, we lose a sense of who we are and what should be important in our lives. Celebrations make us more aware and symbols help to remember what is not tangible.

Like some of the other mysteries, Christ's baptism is not of any particular mysterious nature unique from other baptisms by St. John, other than circumstances surrounding this particular event. This event is important by its symbolism of Jesus' acceptance of St. John the Baptist's efforts to prepare followers for the Baptism of the Spirit into a new life, a new direction, a new covenant, that is eternal. Our baptism of water is symbolic of this new life, one that begins with this moment and continues unending through and beyond death.

The mysterious circumstances surrounding his Baptism may be best described by quoting St. Matthew's Gospel 3:16-17: "And when Jesus had been baptized, he immediately came up from the water. And behold, the heavens were opened to him, and he saw the Spirit of God descending as a dove and coming upon him. And behold, a voice from the heavens said, 'This is my beloved son, in whom I am well pleased.'" It is interesting that these things happened "to him" and "he saw." Only John the Evangelist's Gospel indicates that John the Baptist ". . . bore witness, saying, 'I beheld the Spirit descending as a dove from heaven, and it abode upon him . . . . But he who sent me to baptize with water said to me, He upon whom thou wilt see the Spirit descending, . . . he it is who baptizes with the Holy Spirit.'" John 1:32-33. None of the Gospels indicate that anyone in particular was present other than Jesus and John, but John's Gospel does say that, as Jesus approached John that day, John the Baptist said: "'Behold, the lamb of God, who takes away the sin of the world! This is he of whom I said, After me there comes one who has been set above me, . . .'" John 1:29-30. Since John is talking about Jesus as the third person, he must have been talking to someone other than Jesus, implying that there was one or more others present. What this means is that there was someone there besides John to pass on to the writer of the Gospel what they witnessed. John the Baptist had little time left on earth.

What, in fact, did Jesus and John and anyone else actually see that day when the Spirit of God was descending as a dove and the heavens opened up? For the lack of information, it leaves a lot up to our imaginations.

2. The Wedding Feast of Cana.

This event was the first of many miracles Jesus performed during the following three years of his ministry. At Cana he did not heal the sick, cure the lame, bring eyesight to the blind or return sanity to the spiritually possessed, as he did frequently throughout his ministry. But this was the *first* miracle, and, as one of the mysteries, can represent all of them, for surely, each and every one of his miracles is a mystery to the practical minded, for they defy scientific explanation, even today.

A miracle may be defined in different ways: it can defy the laws of Nature or, by unexpected coincidence or unforeseeable occurrence, something good happens, especially when prayed for or left in the hands of the Almighty. God knows ways that we may never think of, perfectly natural, but, from the standpoint of the one affected, subsequent events bring resolution to a difficult or seemingly impossible situation. This may be called a miracle, irony, or just good fortune, but, when God is in control, anything can happen.

One type of cure that Christ demonstrated was to return sanity to the spiritually possessed, or exorcism. Exorcisms have been performed by highly knowledgeable individuals, usually priests, and can be a long drawn-out process, not instantaneous like the miracles of Christ. It is odd that Satan would make himself so clearly evident by possession when it is said that he prefers to keep his existence unnoticed because he can work more effectively that way. I wonder why video cameras are not used, as witness to his existence.

There was a time when I entertained the belief that evil existed only as the absence of good, or the absence of God, not in the form of devils or fallen angels. After some reevaluation, I see a great deal of intelligent activity or forces that seem to be beyond coincidence, that meddle in our lives in clever ways that lead us toward evil and finding excuses for doing the wrong thing, often based on insufficient evidence. In other words, Satan.

One good example of how some sly hidden intelligence has a way of leading us toward greater evil is what today is called "the slippery slope." Start off with insignificant acts that can be justified by the fact or illusion that it cannot hurt anyone; therefore, it is alright, such as little white lies, petty theft, masturbation, etc. We are blind to how justifying in our minds the little things can so easily lead to slightly bigger things, and little by little, step by step, we find justification for serious things. The seemingly harmless soon leads to vice, bad habits, crime. The slippery slope is easier sliding down than crawling back up. It is easier paddling downstream than paddling back up. Avoiding all temptations to justify the evil from the start can avoid greater problems and guilt later.

Another often overlooked consequence that blindly justifies the small things is how a small personal benefit, that appears to be a mere drop in the ocean, becomes significant if everyone else does it too. If "everyone" cheats on their income taxes (millions of people), the loss translates into significant losses to our government. It hurts not only services to us all, but the honest citizens who do not cheat, not that the government is always innocent in how they use the funds. They, of course, are vulnerable to the slippery slope too.

Especially significant is how huge corporations can avoid paying taxes by finding loopholes. The primary objective of the tax division of the accounting department is to save their employer money. The common good is overlooked and selfish interests send lobbyists to elected officials seeking to sway votes toward their personal gain over the common good . . . . This is getting off the subject.

Christ talked about devils and the Gospels clearly describe Jesus being tempted by Satan. If his temptation passage was only a symbolic story, then where do we draw the line between truth and fiction, between historical record and allegorical story-telling to reveal some truth. This would take us into another issue altogether. How about Christ? Did *he* really exist? I never heard anyone deny that he did.

Another factor that Cana brings to light is that of Mary's relationship with her son. Jesus wasn't ready to begin his ministry quite yet, but due to his mother's insistence he agreed to obey her request to provide for the dwindling supply of wine. Somehow, she knew Jesus could do something, and Jesus' obedience to his mother shows a different degree of respect for her than he demonstrated at age twelve. Jesus' plans were altered by Mary. Mary had influence in Christ's plan. This event brings hope to those who believe in praying to Mary.

3. Proclamation of the Kingdom.

Out of the twenty mysteries, this is the only one that is not applicable to any single event, but to many references made by Jesus throughout his ministry years. The Proclamation of the Kingdom may also be the single most important mystery of them all to me if I, in all honesty, am a self-interested person by my human nature, perhaps selfish, if you will.

Is it not human nature to value self-preservation above all else? The Kingdom is our destiny. It is our ticket to life everlasting. It means that death is the beginning, not the end. The deathbed is a very sad prospect to face for the non-believer. Let's face it: if God says that how we live doesn't matter, that, when we die, it's over and done with, would we really want to serve Him, do His will? Would we care? Each one of us is interested in the self. It's the way God made us, and He knows it. The Kingdom is God's promise. How could we not be grateful? Why would we not wish to serve Him, especially because by doing so we are also doing what is best for ourselves, which is not always apparent. The problem is too often our faith is weak. Then temptation enters in. We cannot see long range consequences, only the foreseeable future. God sees forever.

The other nineteen mysteries are supportive of the Kingdom, some of them essential. But, one may argue, we could eliminate all the others as unneeded. Why not just go right to the eternal joy and forget all the rest? Did Christ have to enter into our world to save us for the Kingdom? Did he have to suffer like he did? Did he have to win the battle over Satan by dying on the Cross? Must we gain the appreciation and knowledge of the Kingdom by the difficult road of living? Well, apparently, God thinks so.

And what is the Kingdom like? It is impossible for any human to comprehend God totally. And it makes sense to me that it should take forever to absorb God. We will never see God in His entirety, because He is infinite. Surely, God does not change, but strengthened at each stage of our lives, we will grow to know and to love Him. Begin today and we will be started, and finally prepared to continue forever when the time comes. This is my theory. Some say there is no time in eternity.

For a simple example, I personally, love to travel. I love to visit and explore places. Exploring and learning about the created physical Universe, with its hundreds of billions of stars in each of hundreds of billions of galaxies, and the array of planets and moons that we are just beginning to discover through astronomy, is going to take me awhile. The time element it took to create what is out there today is just another dimension, along with all the stages of change that took place over the eons of time. Exploring the lives we are living, from start to finish, of every human that ever lived, or will live, could be an exciting adventure too. Exposing to everyone else what I did with my life could be the difference between heaven and hell. Therein lies the purgatory that we all may have to share. And that's for those of us who inhabit just one small planet, just one small electron.

4. The Transfiguration.

Have you ever found yourself sailing through life, when everything seems to be going well, and you see no reason why it should not continue, then bad things start happening? And, when bad things keep coming and there seems to be no end in sight, things start turning around, and you find yourself sailing through life again? . . . Of course, we all do.

Peter, James and his brother John were exhilarated by the extraordinary event of the Transfiguration, followed soon by Christ's Passion and Death on the Cross. Life had taken a turn for the worse. Then, of course, the Resurrection. From the pits to the top. The constant repetition of ups and downs in our lives can seem to go on endlessly to a point that it can become monotonous, but not here.

The Apostles did not want to believe Christ's repeated warnings that he would suffer and die. They were not listening. Christ knew this. For Peter, James and John, the Transfiguration could have been a source of hope for the hard times ahead, but they soon abandoned Christ during his darkest time. Present fear erased their recent memories of this celestial event.

". . . his face shown as the sun, and his garments became as white as snow. And behold there appeared to them Moses and Elijah talking together with him . . . . behold a bright cloud overshadowed them, and behold, a voice out of the cloud said, 'This is my beloved Son, in whom I am well pleased; hear him.'" Matthew 17:2-3,5. Unlike the appearance of the angel at the Annunciation, exactly what they saw here is fairly well described. What is interesting is, like Christ's Baptism, the words from above are the same. At the Baptism the words seem to be identifying to all present who Christ is. At the Transfiguration the voice is reminding and reassuring the three Apostles as to who Christ is. But how soon we forget. What does it take to penetrate our minds and hearts who Christ is and the power he carries during hard times? A constant habit of reinforcing our faith can help.

5. The Institution of the Eucharist.

Throughout Christ's ministry years he taught through parables and by his own example how to live, never teaching ritualistic procedures or specific steps to be taken in a given situation. He wanted us to follow his teachings based on love, a guideline, not a formula. Whatever action contributes toward loving one another is good. But there is one exception where he asked us to follow a specific procedure of worship: the Eucharist, when he said "Do this in memory of me." Luke 22:19.

The Apostles at the Last Supper did not understand the full significance and meaning that the Eucharist would carry, as we in turn would carry with us throughout the centuries. He took bread and wine and said "This is my body" and "this is my blood." It would be "shed for many unto the forgiveness of sins." Matthew 26:26,28. Some Christians, including Catholics and some non-Catholics, believe it is changed physically into the body and blood of Christ, then and today, under the continued appearances of bread and wine. Other non-Catholics believe it is only a symbolic presence.

The Eucharist is very special. In spite of varying beliefs, it is something concrete that Jesus gave us, something to share, something universally affordable and simple, to be a cherished remembrance, that can be done in many different ways as befitting many cultures. The Last Supper was for the Jewish celebration of the Passover, in remembrance of the Israelites' escape from 430 years of slavery under the Egyptian pharaohs. Jesus was dedicated to Judaic customs.

It is the genius of God to institute something so flexible, so meaningful, so powerful, in tying a divided world together . . . in unity. What a beautiful legacy we have! Why did Jesus institute the Eucharist in this form? I think there are many reasons why this form fits. Like the Passion, I cannot invent anything more awesome.

Christ's physical presence is not detectable through the senses. Similarly, the presence of God is not detectable through the senses. He is in another world, a spiritual world. If we can believe in a God we cannot see with our eyes or feel by touch, it should not be so difficult to believe the physical and spiritual presence of Christ's Body and Blood in the host and the cup. The Eucharist brings together the two aspects of God's Kingdom, the one we know in the physical world and the one we will know in eternity.

The Eucharist brings together as one the physical nourishment of bread and wine with the nourishment of our spiritual being through the physical presence of Christ's Body and Blood. Is this not easy to understand? Yes, it is not. Not at all, but it challenges us to reach out for the spiritual world that we, quite honestly, can only understand to a very superficial degree, and will experience more clearly after our current lives are complete.

The Eucharist also brings together a little bit of God's Creation through Nature in the wheat and the grapes through growth and by our participation by planting and harvesting, God and man working together, in unity. The physical and the spiritual are combined in the Eucharist as death blends the two into Eternity. The Eucharist brings us together body and soul at the celebration of community, together, God and men and women, within the confines of church services throughout the world. Any separation between us through race, culture, sex or otherwise is broken by this shared ritual, symbolically, spiritually and physically together.

Is our heavenly life going to be physical or spiritual? Or both? Does any of us really know for sure? We Catholics believe in the resurrection of the body, the implication being it is physical. Or is it a spiritual body, whatever that is? It's fun to set our imaginations into motion over what God has planned for us, but, to know for sure, we must wait.

The conservative has his way, the traditional way, of celebrating the Eucharist. It is meaningful to him. It has been so for Catholics for centuries. For the conservative, it is the right way of doing it. It works.

The liberal has his way, a new way of celebrating the Eucharist. It is meaningful to him, more so than the traditional way. For the liberal it is a better way, a more meaningful way. It works.

The beauty of the Eucharist, the unifying celebration that only God could have dreamed up, is that it, in all its simplicity, can be expressed in an infinite number of variations, in any language, and still maintain the integrity of how he intended at that last supper before he died, a death that is the very essence of the Eucharist celebration itself, a death that would resonate through the centuries. It has become a unifying element for and through us all.

Why would the conservative criticize the liberal or the liberal walk away from his traditions, in complete rejection? It is not right. We should all be celebrating and loving each other and each other's participation in Christ's unifying gift to each and every one of us. All we need to do is accept it, thank God for it and . . . and stop quibbling.

Even for those Protestant churches that celebrate the Eucharist, as they see fit, only as a symbolic presence and not a real physical presence, is that not better than no Eucharist at all? For them in their celebration, it is probably exactly what they believe it to be: symbolic. And God must love them for their devotion. Some Catholics are ready to condemn for not doing it "properly," and vice versa. Why?

Christ came down from the spiritual to us in the physical through his Incarnation and brutal death. He merely asks us to reach up to God in an unbloody way from the physical to the spiritual through the Eucharist by accepting his presence in faith and love and hope for our final reunion with God in eternity.

Sorrowful Mysteries:

Although the Sorrowful Mysteries are sad and painful to think about in their historical reality, they are the most significant and poignant and perhaps beloved of them all. First, they are both clear and unbearably understandable. What Christ endured is beyond our abilities to fully imagine. There have been many unfortunate individuals throughout history who can better relate, based on personal experience. Many have come close or perhaps even gone beyond the physical suffering that Christ endured. Christ's Passion lasted less than one day, but, for some, such as prisoners of Nazi concentration camps or political prisoners, prisoners of war and millions of men, women and children starving through circumstances beyond their control, the torture is daily for weeks, months and even years. The intensity of Christ's concentrated agony, however, may be beyond comparison.

Look into the eyes of an infant: the innocence, the wonder, the curiosity. Someday, that child will accept or reject God, will accept goodness or prefer evil, will grow and learn, love and suffer. Christ was once a child who would someday suffer. And his mother Mary looked lovingly into his eyes, not knowing what the future would bring, as any mother, whether it be that of John the Baptist, Adolph Hitler, or me, or you. What will that innocence, wonder and curiosity turn into? What will he suffer? How will he sin? How will he partake in God's plan? Will those eyes be saved? Or condemned?

Mary must have looked into the baby Jesus' eyes with hope and wonder, never thinking for a moment that he would suffer like he did. At the Presentation, Simeon warned that "a sword thy soul shall pierce." But she could not have understood at that time how this could be. In like manner, mothers throughout history would in hindsight understand the agony of Mary's "pierce" when their child goes off to war, undergoes torture or is lost to starvation. Equally painful is the senseless loss of a child to disease, which could have found a cure had funding and manpower not been diverted to uses devoted to power and greed. Such thoughts can occupy our minds when we pray the Sorrowful Mysteries of the Rosary. The universality of a mother's "pierce" should lay inescapable groundwork for the unity of us all.

I wonder what is the greater sorrow, the loss of a spouse or the loss of a son or daughter? We know little about what happened to Mary's spouse. It is assumed that Joseph died before Jesus' years of ministry. Mary must have experienced the loss of Joseph and now the tragic loss of Jesus. She had to experience both losses. The agony she must have felt during Christ's Passion is well displayed in Mel Gibson's movie "The Passion." How historically accurate his vision of how the Passion affected both Jesus and Mary is hard to say, but what the movie indicates certainly leads me to appreciate how Mary suffered out of love for her son and how Christ suffered for all of us. One should wonder how serious our sins are, how painful they can be to the victims of our transgressions.

An important question about Christ's Passion: did this really happen? It is easy to dismiss something that happened 2000 years ago in our busy modern day world. If Christ never existed, or if the story of his Passion and Resurrection is just a legend, a hoax or just a pat fictitious story creatively concocted and passed on by the early Gospel writers, what good is it? It would just be a meaningful morality story of the love of God, but outside the course of physical reality, a wistful dream of heaven and pleasant destinies. But over and above anyone's doubts, it seems inconceivable that a man would suffer like Christ did, in meek acceptance, if he knows that all that he claims in the Gospels is false. And who could invent such a story?

Furthermore, first century Jewish religious leaders, as well as Jewish historian Josephus, never denied that he existed. Islam respects Christ as a prophet and honors his mother Mary. No one that I am aware of has ever provided a nonexistence theory of Jesus Christ. This kind of theory has little support.

In recent years writings collaborating the Gospels and letters of the New Testament have been found in many caves in the Holy Lands, hidden from unbelievers and persecutors of Christians at the time, then forgotten for centuries. The spirit of Jesus Christ, meanwhile, has been kept alive thanks to the brilliance and universality through time of his teachings that make them work.

What about the claim that Christ, in spite of these mysteries, was not the Messiah? Predictions about the Messiah by prophets in the Old Testament were fulfilled during Christ's life, such as the virgin birth (Isaiah 7:14), the birth of the Messiah in Bethlehem (Michaeus 5:2) and the return from Egypt (Osee 11:11). The slaughter of the Innocents (Jeremias 31:15) was fulfilled, thanks to King Herod, forcing the Holy Family to flee into Egypt. All the prophesies of old are fulfilled. Only the flawed expectations were not. Christ's version of the Messiah did not live up to what Jewish leaders wanted. Christ was someone above and beyond their imaginations.

And why? Why the Passion and Death? But before we take on this difficult question, let us take a look at these five Sorrowful Mysteries and see what they may tell us.

1. The Agony in the Garden.

"Father, if it is possible, let this cup pass away from me; yet not as I will, but as thou willest." (Matthew 26:39). One may ask: how would Matthew know the words of Christ in private prayer? Good question. After the Resurrection, Christ had plenty of time in forty days to converse with his disciples. And keep in mind that the Scriptures were inspired by the Holy Spirit, for how could the ancient prophets prophesy?

Christ's humanity shows through here, as the Son asks the Father to be released from the suffering that he, as divine, knows is about to happen to him. It is interesting to contemplate on the question of how much did Jesus know, how much of the how, in detail, he would be forced to endure. Did he know he would be scourged, that he would be crucified the next day, how painful the nails would be when penetrating through his hands and feet? Like the newborn Jesus, how much does he know now and how much did he know then?

And like his mother at the Annunciation, Jesus, in humility, seconds his will to the will of the Father.

You wonder if Jesus was more in dread of the impending torture than he was anxious to get on with what must be and get it over with. And, if he must suffer, did he look forward joyfully to save us from our sins because of his great love for the Father and for all of us?

As Jesus agonizes alone, disciples are not far off, with little apparent awareness of what was in store for Jesus the next day, and little apparent awareness of their own fears and cowardice that would lead them to abandon their master, something they thought they would never do. We all can be fearless in our minds until the peril becomes real. Then, . . . who knows? Premeditated fearlessness could bring about an immediate surge of bravery to react in a given situation, if one doesn't have much time to think. Awareness of consequences from authorities in a dictatorial existence can cause fear that those who have only known the benefits of freedom and justice cannot fully appreciate.

Peter's sudden reaction to Jesus' arrest by cutting off the ear of the high priest's servant was one of anger and only detrimental to Jesus' way of nonviolence, and the fulfillment of prophecy. "In that hour Jesus said to the crowds, 'As against a robber you have come out, with swords and clubs, to seize me. I sat daily with you in the temple teaching, and you did not lay hands on me.'" (Matthew 26:55). Without a crowd of followers surrounding him as in the temple, the armed crowd came at night against little opposition. Although cowardice is not unique, powerful regimes have been brought down by the courage of the people, usually people who have been pushed too far, who have little to lose, but all too often it comes in the form of violence.

2. Scourging at the Pillar.

The physical torture begins. Jesus has been judged by the angry mob, spurred on by envious Jewish religious leaders. The procurator in charge reluctantly lets go to their pressure. He is torn between his conscience and his fear from pressure of a riot breaking out. His position is at stake from Roman authorities. His fears win out.

All this fulfills scriptural prophesy. How guilty are they who are actually fulfilling the course of history as prophesied? How guilty was Judas in his prophesied betrayal? Could they resist the wrong that they did? Or are they pawns in the hands of prophesy? Was Judas' character known to Jesus before he was chosen as one of the twelve? Was that why he was chosen? If not them, prophesy may have been carried out some other way. Those participants of injustice are likely steeped in weakness and sin to begin with. But only God can judge.

I have never been scourged. Have you? I don't know how many lashes, what the whip may have been made of, or how brutal was the torturer. I can only imagine, and should. I was not there . . . . But Jesus was.

3. Crowning of Thorns.

Where the scourging was a suffering by physical pain, the Crowning of Thorns was mostly a suffering through humiliation. He was placed in the hands of Pilate's soldiers and they stripped him, crowned him with a ring made of thorns, physically painful in itself, mocked him as King of the Jews, spat on him and struck him on the head. Jesus, the Son of God, took all this without reaction. Meanwhile, the wounds from the scourging are smarting and bleeding. I wonder how those soldiers will feel on Judgment Day when they find out who it was they were mocking and spitting on: "Oh."

You wonder how humans can take pleasure in hurting another. Is it a feeling of pride? Superiority? Perhaps an outlet for their own feelings of inferiority? An outlet for frustrations of their own? Maybe they were trained to be mean and tough in order to carry out their duties as soldiers, and it was the only mentality they knew, like attack dogs. Maybe they thought they were just having fun. Man's inhumanity to man was not unique in those times. Will it ever end? And Jesus forgives. Can we?

4. Carrying of the Cross.

Jesus' suffering continues, both of physical pain and humiliation, as he is forced to carry his own Cross of execution to the place of execution, as was customary for condemned persons of the day, through the streets of Jerusalem and up the slope to Calvary. You wonder what people are thinking that Friday morning as this bloodied man quietly carries on by. Passersby probably turned the other way. Did they have the slightest suspicion that he was God, Creator of their very selves and the Universe?

Jesus, a strong young man, in his prime, a veteran of many long journeys back and forth across what is Israel and Palestine today, by foot, can only take so much, falling three times along the way. Do the soldiers give him a break by letting Simon of Cyrene take over the burden for a while? Or do they fear that Jesus might die before reaching his destiny of the most grotesque torture of all?

The agony last night, the brutal scourging, the humiliating mockery are all behind him. Each step takes Jesus closer to Calvary. Does Jesus long for that destination to get it over with? Or does he plod along with impending dread? Or torn between both? Each step becomes another that he would never have to make, but each step adds weariness to the next one.

Think of Mary's feelings as she witnesses her bloodied son on that public street. How much has she been aware of? Where was she last night? Did she know he was in prison? Did she know where he was this morning? Was she present when the crowds called for his crucifixion? Was she looking for him? Finding him now is not the same as finding him in the temple twenty years ago . . . . Does she remember Simeon's words of prophesy 32 years ago: "thy own soul a sword shall pierce"? According to Gibson's movie she was well aware of the proceedings from the arrest and throughout but was hopelessly unable to do anything about it. She was probably reminded by Jesus more than once of this impending destiny and the need to fulfill the prophesies of Scripture. Christ carried the weight of our sins on his shoulders that day. We participate in this scene in one of two ways by our thoughts, words and actions: we are shoulders or we are crosses. What contributions do I make?

5. The Crucifixion.

Jesus has arrived. His active physical participation is over. His passive participation remains. All he must do is let others do it to him. The executioners will see to that. What remains is the climax, the ultimate torture of the day piled over his racked body. Can any of us conceive what that initial penetration of heavy nail must feel like on one hand, and then the other, and finally through both feet? And the stress on aching bones, the stretching muscles and ligaments, the shredded skin, as he is lifted into place, all his weight supported off at least three concentrated points, for three hours? (The exact number of nails is not known for certain.) That's three long hours! Or 10,800 excruciating seconds. Meanwhile, the derision from onlookers continues. What does it take for a strong young man in good health to die?

"'Father, forgive them, for they do not know what they are doing.'"

He understands us. He forgives us. He has unified divinity with man. He has shed his blood for us. All of it . . . . "'It is consummated.'" John 19:30.

In the Apostles' Creed it is said that Christ, after he died, descended into hell, or to the dead, to release the dead unto life. But, in Luke 23:43, he said to the good thief: "this day thou shalt be with me in paradise." The question then is can Jesus be in two places at the same time? Well, if Christ is divine and God is everywhere, then the answer to the question is simple: yes.

So, why do we have to be saved? Are we pawns in the struggle between God and Satan? Good, Love, God vs. evil, hate, Satan? We never asked for this, but we are in the game, a very serious game it seems to me. And save us from what? Damnation. Christ referred to this many times. The choices we make now will determine our destiny. Our eternal destiny! O my God! . . . And Padre Pio says "Don't worry"?

The influences we encounter through life all have an affect on our choices. Influences vary greatly from one person to another. The recruiting job for good and the one for evil that I am exposed to can make all the difference. Lucky are those of us who encounter the ones that lead to the right choices. How we respond to the Natural Law of conscience will determine the degree of responsibility for our choices we shall bear. The fairness lies in God's mercy. Those who are blessed with the better recruiting are given the greater responsibility to serve. We are recruited, we choose whom we wish to serve and it's off to the boot camp of life to learn and to teach others.

In addition to external influences, we have an internal one: as human, we have a conscience. It can tell each of us the difference between right and wrong, the difference between selflessness and selfishness, the difference between long term goals and short. As we mature, external influences can make us aware that what is good for all is inevitably good for me. What goes around, comes around. It's common sense. God's laws are all common sense. Even loving our enemies: what better way to have an effective and profound influence on them. Life's experiences can be a teacher for all of us if we value patience, honesty and humility.

We must learn who we are, the created, and who God is, the Creator: we, the limited and flawed; God, the infinite and perfect. Yet God has invited us all to share His Truth and Love forever, but we must develop the right attitude to receive and accept Him.

If we fail, do we get another chance after this one? Hindus believe in reincarnation. Catholics believe in purgatory, but purgatory is like a finishing process to prepare us for heaven. It is not permanent. Reject God's Truth and Love and we may never get to either.

If Jesus Christ was God, why did he suffer? It is incomprehensible. It may be this incomprehensibility that reveals it a divine plan. Who could have devised such a scenario, one that is so unique, so dramatic, so powerful, yet so ironic, that only God could have come up with it. Even Satan, in spite of his grand intelligence, never saw it coming. Easter Sunday morning Jesus Christ returns to life. I cannot invent anything better. It is perfect, even, I dare say, beautiful.

I honestly do not fully understand what it means that Christ suffered for our sins, all our sins, everyone's. That means that in less than 24 hours, Jesus suffered enough to cover the sins of billions of people that have lived before Christ and 2000 years since so far and more to come. This is not to question the truth of it, since Christ stated it would so be during his lifetime. I just have difficulty in truly understanding it. Perhaps I always have. How does one equate amount of suffering with number and severity of sins? But that is the mystery. It is not for me to understand it, but to accept it. The intensity of his suffering cannot be questioned. For most of us, it can only be imagined, and even then, only inadequately. How much physical? How much psychological? How much spiritual? No one can share fully in his experience; only in our imaginations. Hopefully, nothing more.

He seemed to welcome it through his acceptance. As a man, he asked for relief of this mandate, but accepted the Father's plan. As God, He knew it must be. This grand expression of love overrides any failure on my part to understand. The physical pain alone, out of love, is something I can at least begin to understand as the ultimate human sacrifice of agony and death . . . for my sake.

Glorious Mysteries:

Like the Sorrowful Mysteries, the Glorious are problematic to nonbelievers simply because of the question of whether or not they really happened. They are difficult to prove now 2000 years after the fact. There were witnesses to Christ's presence after he died, but only followers of his teachings. The last three Mysteries do not even involve Jesus, but his disciples and his mother Mary. The descent of the Holy Spirit shows through the inspired actions of Apostles and disciples in years to follow. The glorious events of the last two involve Mary, and proof rests on the conclusions of the Church many years later.

There are several prophesies surrounding the death of Jesus, including: what they offered him to drink on the Cross (Ps 21:16; John 19:29); that they would pierce his side (Zacharias 12:10; John 19:34,37) instead of breaking the bones of his legs, the usual method of final execution to verify death: "The Lord guards all his bones: not even one of them shall be broken" (Ps 33:21; John 19:33); that the soldiers would cast lots for his garments (Ps 21:19; John 19:24). Yet, there is no impartial documentation by nonbelievers who were there of any of these events or any of the Glorious Mysteries to verify that they ever happened. To know anything conclusively that far back in history becomes like anything else, a matter of faith.

Like the Joyful Mystery of the Annunciation, there is one characteristic common to all five Glorious Mysteries: the curiosity they bring to mind regarding the actual event that witnesses did see. Much is left up to the imagination. Images portrayed in paintings may give rise to the images we may have accepted when meditating on them, but how they actually happened are in themselves loaded with mystery. An image of some kind, from the imagination of an artist, is important, whether it be accurate or not, to facilitate meditation.

1. The Resurrection.

Without Christ's death, the Resurrection could not have happened, and without the Resurrection, Christ's death would have little meaning. They work hand-in-hand to generate the phenomenon of Christ's victory over death. It symbolizes and reassures the fulfillment of hope we all share in bringing self-preservation into our lives. They were works of God, works that only the Almighty, God, Allah, Yahweh, could accomplish. From the Resurrection springs Christianity.

One of the great wonders of life is the moment of joy that follows a period of immense trial. How grand it must have been for Christ's disciples to realize this turn of events that took place after Christ's Crucifixion and Death. The one in whom they had put their hearts and souls was gone. Their leader who brought so much meaning and wonder into their lives was now taken away. They did not understand. They did not listen to Christ's forewarnings. Like other Jews, their vision of the Messiah was not in tune to God's plan. Who would have known what was about to happen? And then Sunday morning: the thrill, the unfolding of new meaning, the uplifting from their pain, the beginning, not the end. "Jesus said to her, 'Mary!'" (John 20:16). All that was needed was a jumpstart to remove their fears of current religious and political pressure.

Like death unto life everlasting, we can work toward that destiny by inclusion in God's Kingdom now by our lives today. The fetus lives in its womb as it grows toward its birth unto the world outside, perhaps quite comfortable in its familiar surroundings, not wanting to go anywhere else. It is not ready . . . . We are comfortable to go on living our present lives, not wanting to die. We are not ready . . . . Little does the fetus know of the destiny that lies ahead, until it cannot grow any further, its purpose in the womb is complete, and must escape from the confinement and vision of the womb, and be born into a wondrous new world, one that will accommodate a new stage of growth and wonder . . . . We must eventually escape the womb of this life and be born into eternal life and the wonder of God's love for us (taken from a funeral homily by Father Tom Lumpkin of Detroit).

We preview this birth into eternal life by our inclusion in God's Kingdom now. We are reborn by putting our hearts and souls into Scripture, Christ's teachings, and guidance of the Holy Spirit. We must be like children, and listen.

The only ones present at the moment of the Resurrection were the soldiers guarding the tomb. They reported this to the Jewish religious leaders and were not to tell anyone and were paid to say the disciples "stole him" (Matthew 28:13). Why the religious leaders could not weigh in the possibility of Jesus as their Savior by this time makes one wonder about their sincerity. They wouldn't dare to accept it now after what they did to him. Yet, you wonder too how Matthew new all this. He was not there. Who told him? The soldiers? The religious leaders? Or the Holy Spirit? Jews today can easily point to this to justify their disbelief.

2. The Ascension.

Christ's disciples were present at this unique event. There were plenty of witnesses, but little documentation. ". . . as he blessed them, . . . he parted from them and was carried up into heaven" (Luke 24:51). What did they actually see: "carried *up*"? Physically or figuratively? Did he actually rise up into the sky? Into a cloud? Heaven isn't up there in the clouds someplace, is it? So what *did* they see?

I have always pictured Jesus levitating toward the sky and fading away, like a disappearing ghost in the movies. Maybe that's what Christ did, like an artist's painting that we have seen, the only image of going to heaven that his primitive astronomical knowledge would allow him to understand. But one would think it was something else. The Gospels do not elaborate. But in Acts 1:9-10, it is written: ". . . he was lifted up before their eyes and a cloud took him out of their sight. And . . . they were gazing up to heaven as he went." This confusing implication that heaven is in a physical location somewhere up in the sky begs for explanation I cannot provide.

3. The Descent of the Holy Spirit upon the Apostles.

Faith is a gift. It is not something we can achieve, like working toward a college degree, or a financial nest egg for retirement. One can discover through research, or schooling, or even brainwashing by parents or teachers, or other means of exposure, but to believe the truth over and above all other influences we encounter is truly a gift. Making the right choice among all those influences may be impossible without the guidance of a higher force.

Even after witnessing Christ's Death and Resurrection, the influence of Christ's presence with the disciples was not enough after the Ascension. Jesus' physical presence was gone. Their faith was still weak as they hid from authorities in spite of Christ's instruction to "Go . . . and make disciples of all nations, . . ." (Matthew 28:19). The gift of faith came to them through the third Glorious Mystery.

When Jesus was about to ascend into heaven, he said ". . . you shall be baptized with the Holy Spirit not many days hence." (Acts 1:5). It turned out to be ten days. See Acts 2:1-4. There were 120 present: Apostles and disciples, including women. After this miraculous moment they fearlessly went out and preached to the people, who heard them in each of their own diverse languages, of which there were many. Three thousand were converted that day (see Acts 2:41), both a miracle and a mystery.

The Holy Spirit has continued His inspiration through missionaries and martyrs and each one of us. It is the Holy Spirit, the Third Person of the one God that inspires all of us through music, entertainment, philosophy, architecture, art, scientific research and development, teaching, child rearing, charity, whatever is good. Are our accomplishments a source of pride on our part? Or are they more accurately a cause for thanksgiving? The passion that drives us can be credited to exposure, interest, inspiration and opportunity; all dependent on the will of God through the Holy Spirit. We can find much joy in being a part of God's Kingdom, now and forever.

The Holy Spirit works through us throughout the ages. It is a challenge for us to sort out what is the good and what is not, not what is liberal or what is conservative. Both have a responsibility to play a part.

4. The Assumption.

Once again, what did those present witness as Mary made the transition into heaven, both soul and body, immediately after death? Did her body disappear? There are no known relics of her body nor has there been any search by the early Church for such items. This brings us to one of the primary arguments for the Assumption belief: tradition and consensus throughout two millenniums of the Catholic Church. Although the New Testament lacks clear evidence, early writers and preachers referred to it, and they lived more closely to the time of her life, so they would be more attune to evidence passed down on this matter than anyone today 2000 years later.

The Assumption has been touched upon by notable theologians throughout the years, including Pope Leo IV, St. John Damascene, St. Germanus of Constantinople, Bishop Amadeus of Lausarme, St. Anthony of Padua, St. Albert the Great, St. Bernadine of Sienna, St. Robert Bellarmine, St. Francis de Sales, St. Alphonsus and St. Peter Canisius. Each one has been included as references in Pope Pius XII's "Munificentissimus Deus," the Apostolic Constitution defining the dogma of the Assumption as infallible. (See chapter on "Infallibility".)

For example, St. Alphonsus wrote: "Jesus did not wish to have the body of Mary corrupted after death, since it would have redounded to his own dishonor to have her own virginal flesh, from which he himself had assumed flesh, reduced to dust." This conclusion seems ok except that who am I or Alphonsus to assume the mind of Jesus, a dangerous adventure by mere mortals. This argument, more of opinion than of proof, falls short of certitude, as does many of the other arguments in Pope Pius XII's document. That is *my* opinion, unqualified as it may be. There is no convincing evidence in Scripture to either favor or deny the Assumption that I am aware of.

Pope Pius XII adds point 47: "It is forbidden to any man to change this, our declaration, pronouncement, definition or, by rash attempt, to oppose and counter it. If any man should presume to make such an attempt, let him know that he will incur the wrath of Almighty God and Blessed Apostles Peter and Paul." I dare not want to test his words should he be right, because surely the pope has enormous powers to be able to dictate such reactions from the above mentioned parties. The attitude of Pius's threat reveals a God more of anger than of love and mercy. I doubt God intends us to believe under pressure of fear. "No one is condemned whose refuge is God." Psalms 34:23 (New American Bible).

So what does this all boil down to? How does the Assumption affect the lives of you and me? Will the fact that the body of Mary, the Mother of the Second Person of the Blessed Trinity, has never suffered deterioration and was taken directly into the eternal bliss of heaven at death, going to make me a better person, a happier person? Will it expand my understanding and appreciation of God and His law of love that I must grasp and follow?

Am I missing something? At this point in time I fail to see this as little more than a matter between God and Mary. It is interesting to contemplate, but whether it is true or not will not change my faith in any way, although it may provide hope for my own resurrection and eternal reward. The Church has declared it to be infallibly true by Pope Pius XII, and that's ok with me. I seek only a universal understanding that may lead to greater unity, not to be declared a heretic.

5. The Coronation of Mary Queen of Heaven.

Keep in mind this mystery has not yet been declared "ex cathedra," or infallible, and, therefore, will not appear on the list that does not exist. (See chapter on "Infallibility.")

What constitutes a coronation? Is this some grand demonstrative event that, in this case, takes place in heaven, one showing pomp and glory to Mary, who had set an example of love, humility and patience while enduring great suffering during her life? Is it similar to the coronation of the Queen of England, parading before thousands of well-wishers? This picture, I think, is highly unlikely. The human well-wishers would be few in number if our bodies are not resurrected until the end of time. Perhaps this was intended only for God and the angels, but there is much that we do not understand. That is why it is a mystery.

This event, if it was an event, is one that nonbelievers would probably have fun with. For one thing, how, they might argue, can anyone know that such a thing ever occurred, if no one ever went to heaven and returned to tell about it? Can we rely on the argument that this information has been passed down through divine inspiration? Not too convincing to an atheist. But are we called to defend our faith to an atheist? . . . Yes. I would suggest that the Coronation of Mary takes place through the love of God and the love in our hearts, if for no other reason than for the enormous role she played in Christ's life.

The Coronation could also be a state of existence granted Mary at the instant of the her Assumption: an assumed state of honor, real but not an event.

One may ask: what does her state of being Queen of Heaven mean to you or me, or for Mary for that matter? Traditional Catholics will pray to

Mary with full confidence that their prayer will be answered, and many will attest to her loyalty. She has been a road of access to her son for such requests, a privilege attributed to other saints as well.

The Coronation belief is not a matter of ex cathedra, but a rite of veneration, and not worship toward images that represent her. It is a practice that became popular toward the end of the 16th century and grew in popularity in the United States before Vatican II. Mary was a humble person: the Coronation may mean more to Catholics than it does to her. To the progressive Catholic, Mary's Coronation may mean very little. They have concerns more related to the world that we see.

Overview:

Within each one of twenty Mysteries there can be found a lesson that relates in some specific way to our lives that brings direction and hope. Like Padre Pio says: "Don't worry." In spite of his encouragement, I confess: I worry. Hopefully, we will someday find the courage to put all problems into perspective and find hope in all facets and stages of life.

Prayer can take many forms. It is hard for me to believe that whatever form we choose, God will not be listening with our best interests when we devote the time and have the sincerety to entreat Him. Prayer, alone, like with Jesus in his Agony in the Garden, or in a group, like Jesus said when two or more are gathered in his name, he is in our midst, God is listening. Prayer can take the form of a disciplined repetition, like the rosary or prayer wheels in eastern religions, or of absorbing ourselves in deep philosophical readings, discussion or meditation, or of emptying our thoughts and letting the wanderings of the mind listen with open heart to messages from the Holy Spirit, or of each day doing whatever we do as an offering in service to the Almighty, or whatever. In each form, let Scripture, advice from others and the Natural Law of our conscience be our guides. Prayer can be more than requests. It can be thanksgiving, or praise and adoration in the wonder of His Creation or repentance for the wrongs we have committed. But, above all, sincerity is the key. Every effort is mercifully received. An all-loving God would do no less.

CONCLUSION

Once a rumor starts, suspicion develops into legend. People believe what they want. The way this world is going, division is bound to increase. I feel badly for us all. It could reach a point where passions, fueled by fears of losing eternity to damnation, by nationalistic fervor, by general misunderstanding and the such, will run amok. Vast destruction on both sides will grow out of it and evil powers that be will have won a major victory. Or will the power of God miraculously bring such devastation to a stop? Or will He work through each one of us by our searching tirelessly for the unity of us all?

One source of our search to begin seeking some unity between sides is by eliminating nonessential elements that divide us. So many of the walls that we have built against the enemy are dividing issues that are simply that, just more elements that define division. These are elements that, if we take a close look at them, are insignificant: like what we eat, how we worship, and any number of daily personal habits and beliefs. To each his own, as long as we don't impose hardship or hurt on anyone else. Christ said " 'I desire mercy, and not sacrifice, . . .' " (Matthew 9:13 and 12:7).

To sum up my message, I refer to Pope Francis I's book "Evangelii Gaudium" on page 111, paragraph 228: "This requires acknowledging a principle indispensable to the building of friendship in society: namely, that unity is greater than conflict." In fact, read the whole paragraph. In fact, read all of chapter 4. It is fabulous. In fact, read the whole book.

"For I have come to set a man at variance with his father, and a daughter with her mother, and a daughter-in-law with her mother-in-law; and a man's enemies will be those of his own household. He who loves father or mother more than me is not worthy of me; . . ." (Matthew 10:35-37). Here Christ is not favoring separation over unity. He is stressing unity with God's Truth, even if it means separation from loved ones who deny God's Truth.

God wants us to realize our responsibility in working toward finding his Truth through each other. It can be generosity in giving or it can be humility in receiving. That is His Kingdom, a kingdom of loving. We need a bridge to span over the evils of separation. Christ conquered evil by his sacrifice on the Cross. It is up to us to accept God's Truth and build bridges to others over the waters of separation.

Where will we find the coming of the Anti-Christ? He will rise out of the great abyss of division that will have grown out of this separation between sides. Two sides? Actually, many sides of conflict in the world, us and them, on multiple fronts, each speaking out among themselves against the other, spirited by anger, misunderstanding and ignorance and coupled with those who value power and greed over righteousness. Out of the dark chasm we are creating, the Anti-Christ will come to fill it up with an Armageddon of destruction, hate and horror.

Any dialogue these foregoing words may inspire I hope will be a benefit towards greater unity in a world that is much in need of it. Such dialogue may begin by driving us further apart, but in the long run will help create mutual understanding that can bring us little by little closer together and closer to God, who is Truth itself.

Why does God allow conflicts to exist? Conflicts exist to help us understand a more complex world so that we may expand and intensify our love for each other. A shallow love based on similarity is not as strong and vibrant as one based on diversity. If we turn away from growing into the other world, we are turning away from the greater more diversified world of Love, which is God itself.

Truth and Love are in unity. One is dependent on the other and vice versa.

ABOUT THE AUTHOR

The author was born in Detroit, Michigan, in 1943, graduated from the University of Detroit in 1967 with a bachelor's degree in Architecture and retired in 2005 after a career in Architectural Engineering and Design. A lifetime of interest in photography, cinematography, philosophy, music, travel and athletics has paralleled his spiritual growth through the years. As an amateur moviemaker, he spends much of his retirement editing productions that reflect his various interests. Exercising his interests have led him to publish in 2011 "Pray for Today," a book of prayers and photographs, and now he has expressed his concern for a divided world by publishing "Unity," that explores his vision of how the lack of unity and understanding has penetrated many facets of society. Comments are welcome: REMAKARA@YAHOO.COM.